THE
CORPORATE
MATCHMAKER
JOURNAL

Copyright © 2021 by Ultimate Publishing House

Corporate Matchmaker Journal
By Martin Rowinski

THE ULTIMATE PUBLISHING HOUSE (UPH)
Canadian Office: 205 Glen Shields Avenue
Toronto, Ontario,
Canada L4K 2B0
Telephone: 647-883-1758

CorporateMatchmakerBook.com

www.ultimatepublishinghouse.com
E-mail: info@ultimatepublishinghouse.com

Quantity discounts are available on bulk purchases of this book for reselling, educational
purposes, subscription incentives, gifts, sponsorship, or fundraising. Unique books or book
excerpts can also be fashioned to suit special needs such as private labeling with your logo
on the cover and a message from or a message printed on the second page of the book.

For more information, please contact our Special Sales Department at
Ultimate Publishing House. Orders for college textbook or course adoption use.
Please contact Ultimate Publishing House Tel: 647-883-1758

Corporate Matchmaker Journal-By Martin Rowinski
ISBN: 978-1-7354831-6-0

*"He who is not courageous enough to take risks
will accomplish nothing in life."*

—MUHAMMAD ALI

_____

Here are the Traits of the GREATS required to choose your superstar board members:

- Integrity
- Honesty
- Loyalty
- Respectfulness
- Responsibility

- Humility
- Compassion
- Fairness
- Forgiveness
- Authenticity

Gratitude is key and visualizing in the present moment, exactly what you hold in your mind's eye, take 2 minutes to visualize your board members, in the present tense and feel it in you heart as if the goal is already complete.

TOP THREE THINGS YOU ARE GREATFUL FOR:

1. _____
2. _____
3. _____

FOCUS ON YOUR ONE THING TODAY & TAKE MASSIVE ACTION!

"You can have anything you want if you want it badly enough. You can be anything you want to be, do anything you set out to accomplish if you hold to that desire with singleness of purpose."

—ABRAHAM LINCOLN

―――――――

Here are the Traits of the GREATS required to choose your superstar board members:

- Integrity
- Honesty
- Loyalty
- Respectfulness
- Responsibility

- Humility
- Compassion
- Fairness
- Forgiveness
- Authenticity

Gratitude is key and visualizing in the present moment, exactly what you hold in your mind's eye, take 2 minutes to visualize your board members, in the present tense and feel it in you heart as if the goal is already complete.

TOP THREE THINGS YOU ARE GREATFUL FOR:

1. _____
2. _____
3. _____

FOCUS ON YOUR ONE THING TODAY & TAKE MASSIVE ACTION!

"Here I am . . . wanting to accomplish something and completely forgetting it must all end—that there is such a thing as death."

—LEO TOLSTOY

———————

Here are the Traits of the GREATS required to choose your superstar board members:

- Integrity
- Honesty
- Loyalty
- Respectfulness
- Responsibility

- Humility
- Compassion
- Fairness
- Forgiveness
- Authenticity

Gratitude is key and visualizing in the present moment, exactly what you hold in your mind's eye, take 2 minutes to visualize your board members, in the present tense and feel it in you heart as if the goal is already complete.

TOP THREE THINGS YOU ARE GREATFUL FOR:

1. _____
2. _____
3. _____

FOCUS ON YOUR ONE THING TODAY & TAKE MASSIVE ACTION!

"Knowing is not enough; we must apply.
Willing is not enough; we must do."

—JOHANN WOLFGANG VON GOETHE

———————

Here are the Traits of the GREATS required to choose your superstar board members:

- Integrity
- Honesty
- Loyalty
- Respectfulness
- Responsibility

- Humility
- Compassion
- Fairness
- Forgiveness
- Authenticity

Gratitude is key and visualizing in the present moment, exactly what you hold in your mind's eye, take 2 minutes to visualize your board members, in the present tense and feel it in you heart as if the goal is already complete.

TOP THREE THINGS YOU ARE GREATFUL FOR:

1. _____
2. _____
3. _____

FOCUS ON YOUR ONE THING TODAY & TAKE MASSIVE ACTION!

"Do you want to know who you are? Don't ask. Act!
Action will delineate and define you."

—THOMAS JEFFERSON

———————

Here are the Traits of the GREATS required to choose your superstar board members:

- Integrity
- Honesty
- Loyalty
- Respectfulness
- Responsibility

- Humility
- Compassion
- Fairness
- Forgiveness
- Authenticity

Gratitude is key and visualizing in the present moment, exactly what you hold in your mind's eye, take 2 minutes to visualize your board members, in the present tense and feel it in you heart as if the goal is already complete.

TOP THREE THINGS YOU ARE GREATFUL FOR:

1. _____
2. _____
3. _____

FOCUS ON YOUR ONE THING TODAY & TAKE MASSIVE ACTION!

"The path to success is to take massive, determined actions."

—TONY ROBBINS

———————

Here are the Traits of the GREATS required to choose your superstar board members:

- Integrity
- Honesty
- Loyalty
- Respectfulness
- Responsibility

- Humility
- Compassion
- Fairness
- Forgiveness
- Authenticity

Gratitude is key and visualizing in the present moment, exactly what you hold in your mind's eye, take 2 minutes to visualize your board members, in the present tense and feel it in you heart as if the goal is already complete.

TOP THREE THINGS YOU ARE GREATFUL FOR:

1. _____
2. _____
3. _____

FOCUS ON YOUR ONE THING TODAY & TAKE MASSIVE ACTION!

"Ambition is the path to success.
Persistence is the vehicle you arrive in."

—BILL BRADLEY

———————

Here are the Traits of the GREATS required to choose your superstar board members:

- Integrity
- Honesty
- Loyalty
- Respectfulness
- Responsibility

- Humility
- Compassion
- Fairness
- Forgiveness
- Authenticity

Gratitude is key and visualizing in the present moment, exactly what you hold in your mind's eye, take 2 minutes to visualize your board members, in the present tense and feel it in you heart as if the goal is already complete.

TOP THREE THINGS YOU ARE GREATFUL FOR:

1. _____
2. _____
3. _____

FOCUS ON YOUR ONE THING TODAY & TAKE MASSIVE ACTION!

"Ambition is enthusiasm with a purpose."

—FRANK TYGER

———————

Here are the Traits of the GREATS required to choose your superstar board members:

- Integrity
- Honesty
- Loyalty
- Respectfulness
- Responsibility

- Humility
- Compassion
- Fairness
- Forgiveness
- Authenticity

Gratitude is key and visualizing in the present moment, exactly what you hold in your mind's eye, take 2 minutes to visualize your board members, in the present tense and feel it in you heart as if the goal is already complete.

TOP THREE THINGS YOU ARE GREATFUL FOR:

1. _____
2. _____
3. _____

FOCUS ON YOUR ONE THING TODAY & TAKE MASSIVE ACTION!

*"A man's worth is no greater
than his ambitions."*

—MARCUS AURELIUS

———————

Here are the Traits of the GREATS required to choose your superstar board members:

- Integrity
- Honesty
- Loyalty
- Respectfulness
- Responsibility

- Humility
- Compassion
- Fairness
- Forgiveness
- Authenticity

Gratitude is key and visualizing in the present moment, exactly what you hold in your mind's eye, take 2 minutes to visualize your board members, in the present tense and feel it in you heart as if the goal is already complete.

TOP THREE THINGS YOU ARE GREATFUL FOR:

1. _____
2. _____
3. _____

FOCUS ON YOUR ONE THING TODAY & TAKE MASSIVE ACTION!

"Believe it can be done. When you believe something can be done, really believe, your mind will find the ways to do it. Believing a solution paves the way to solution."

—DAVID JOSEPH SCHWARTZ

————————

Here are the Traits of the GREATS required to choose your superstar board members:

- Integrity
- Honesty
- Loyalty
- Respectfulness
- Responsibility

- Humility
- Compassion
- Fairness
- Forgiveness
- Authenticity

Gratitude is key and visualizing in the present moment, exactly what you hold in your mind's eye, take 2 minutes to visualize your board members, in the present tense and feel it in you heart as if the goal is already complete.

TOP THREE THINGS YOU ARE GREATFUL FOR:

1. _____
2. _____
3. _____

FOCUS ON YOUR ONE THING TODAY & TAKE MASSIVE ACTION!

"Be brave to stand for what you
believe in even if you stand alone."

—ROY T. BENNETT

———————

Here are the Traits of the GREATS required to choose your superstar board members:

- Integrity
- Honesty
- Loyalty
- Respectfulness
- Responsibility

- Humility
- Compassion
- Fairness
- Forgiveness
- Authenticity

Gratitude is key and visualizing in the present moment, exactly what you hold in your mind's eye, take 2 minutes to visualize your board members, in the present tense and feel it in you heart as if the goal is already complete.

TOP THREE THINGS YOU ARE GREATFUL FOR:

1. _____
2. _____
3. _____

FOCUS ON YOUR ONE THING TODAY & TAKE MASSIVE ACTION!

"Believing in yourself is not for you; it's for every person who has touched your life in a significant way and for every person your life will touch the same way five minutes from now, or five centuries from now."

—JAYE MILLER

Here are the Traits of the GREATS required to choose your superstar board members:

- Integrity
- Honesty
- Loyalty
- Respectfulness
- Responsibility

- Humility
- Compassion
- Fairness
- Forgiveness
- Authenticity

Gratitude is key and visualizing in the present moment, exactly what you hold in your mind's eye, take 2 minutes to visualize your board members, in the present tense and feel it in you heart as if the goal is already complete.

TOP THREE THINGS YOU ARE GREATFUL FOR:

1. _____

2. _____

3. _____

FOCUS ON YOUR ONE THING TODAY & TAKE MASSIVE ACTION!

"Clarity precedes success."

—ROBIN SHARMA

———————

Here are the Traits of the GREATS required to choose your superstar board members:

- Integrity
- Honesty
- Loyalty
- Respectfulness
- Responsibility

- Humility
- Compassion
- Fairness
- Forgiveness
- Authenticity

Gratitude is key and visualizing in the present moment, exactly what you hold in your mind's eye, take 2 minutes to visualize your board members, in the present tense and feel it in you heart as if the goal is already complete.

TOP THREE THINGS YOU ARE GREATFUL FOR:

1. _____
2. _____
3. _____

FOCUS ON YOUR ONE THING TODAY & TAKE MASSIVE ACTION!

"A lack of clarity could put the brakes
on any journey to success."

—STEVE MARABOLI

———————

Here are the Traits of the GREATS required to choose your superstar board members:

- Integrity
- Honesty
- Loyalty
- Respectfulness
- Responsibility

- Humility
- Compassion
- Fairness
- Forgiveness
- Authenticity

Gratitude is key and visualizing in the present moment, exactly what you hold in your mind's eye, take 2 minutes to visualize your board members, in the present tense and feel it in you heart as if the goal is already complete.

TOP THREE THINGS YOU ARE GREATFUL FOR:

1. _____
2. _____
3. _____

FOCUS ON YOUR ONE THING TODAY & TAKE MASSIVE ACTION!

"Clarity affords focus."

—THOMAS LEONARD

———

Here are the Traits of the GREATS required to choose your superstar board members:

- Integrity
- Honesty
- Loyalty
- Respectfulness
- Responsibility

- Humility
- Compassion
- Fairness
- Forgiveness
- Authenticity

Gratitude is key and visualizing in the present moment, exactly what you hold in your mind's eye, take 2 minutes to visualize your board members, in the present tense and feel it in you heart as if the goal is already complete.

TOP THREE THINGS YOU ARE GREATFUL FOR:

1. _____
2. _____
3. _____

FOCUS ON YOUR ONE THING TODAY & TAKE MASSIVE ACTION!

"The ultimate measure of a man is not where he stands in moments of comfort and convenience, but where he stands at times of challenge and controversy."

—MARTIN LUTHER KING, JR.

———————

Here are the Traits of the GREATS required to choose your superstar board members:

- Integrity
- Honesty
- Loyalty
- Respectfulness
- Responsibility

- Humility
- Compassion
- Fairness
- Forgiveness
- Authenticity

Gratitude is key and visualizing in the present moment, exactly what you hold in your mind's eye, take 2 minutes to visualize your board members, in the present tense and feel it in you heart as if the goal is already complete.

TOP THREE THINGS YOU ARE GREATFUL FOR:

1. _____
2. _____
3. _____

FOCUS ON YOUR ONE THING TODAY & TAKE MASSIVE ACTION!

"The key to life is accepting challenges. Once someone stops doing this, he's dead."

—BETTE DAVIS

———————

Here are the Traits of the GREATS required to choose your superstar board members:

- Integrity
- Honesty
- Loyalty
- Respectfulness
- Responsibility

- Humility
- Compassion
- Fairness
- Forgiveness
- Authenticity

Gratitude is key and visualizing in the present moment, exactly what you hold in your mind's eye, take 2 minutes to visualize your board members, in the present tense and feel it in you heart as if the goal is already complete.

TOP THREE THINGS YOU ARE GREATFUL FOR:

1. _____
2. _____
3. _____

FOCUS ON YOUR ONE THING TODAY & TAKE MASSIVE ACTION!

"I don't run away from a challenge because I am afraid. Instead, I run towards it because the only way to escape fear is to trample it beneath your foot."

—NADIA COMANECI

Here are the Traits of the GREATS required to choose your superstar board members:

- Integrity
- Honesty
- Loyalty
- Respectfulness
- Responsibility

- Humility
- Compassion
- Fairness
- Forgiveness
- Authenticity

Gratitude is key and visualizing in the present moment, exactly what you hold in your mind's eye, take 2 minutes to visualize your board members, in the present tense and feel it in you heart as if the goal is already complete.

TOP THREE THINGS YOU ARE GREATFUL FOR:

1. _____
2. _____
3. _____

FOCUS ON YOUR ONE THING TODAY & TAKE MASSIVE ACTION!

*"Once you have commitment, you need the discipline
and hard work to get you there."*

—HAILE GEBRSELASSIE

Here are the Traits of the GREATS required to choose your superstar board members:

- Integrity
- Honesty
- Loyalty
- Respectfulness
- Responsibility

- Humility
- Compassion
- Fairness
- Forgiveness
- Authenticity

Gratitude is key and visualizing in the present moment, exactly what you hold in your mind's eye, take 2 minutes to visualize your board members, in the present tense and feel it in you heart as if the goal is already complete.

TOP THREE THINGS YOU ARE GREATFUL FOR:

1. _____
2. _____
3. _____

FOCUS ON YOUR ONE THING TODAY & TAKE MASSIVE ACTION!

"Commitment is an act, not a word."

—JEAN-PAUL SARTRE

———————

Here are the Traits of the GREATS required to choose your superstar board members:

- Integrity
- Honesty
- Loyalty
- Respectfulness
- Responsibility

- Humility
- Compassion
- Fairness
- Forgiveness
- Authenticity

Gratitude is key and visualizing in the present moment, exactly what you hold in your mind's eye, take 2 minutes to visualize your board members, in the present tense and feel it in you heart as if the goal is already complete.

TOP THREE THINGS YOU ARE GREATFUL FOR:

1. _____
2. _____
3. _____

FOCUS ON YOUR ONE THING TODAY & TAKE MASSIVE ACTION!

*"Commitment is what transforms
a promise into a reality."*

—ABRAHAM LINCOLN

———————

Here are the Traits of the GREATS required to choose your superstar board members:

- Integrity
- Honesty
- Loyalty
- Respectfulness
- Responsibility

- Humility
- Compassion
- Fairness
- Forgiveness
- Authenticity

Gratitude is key and visualizing in the present moment, exactly what you hold in your mind's eye, take 2 minutes to visualize your board members, in the present tense and feel it in you heart as if the goal is already complete.

TOP THREE THINGS YOU ARE GREATFUL FOR:

1. _____
2. _____
3. _____

FOCUS ON YOUR ONE THING TODAY & TAKE MASSIVE ACTION!

"Optimism is the faith that leads to achievement. Nothing can be done without hope and confidence."

—HELEN KELLER

———————

Here are the Traits of the GREATS required to choose your superstar board members:

- Integrity
- Honesty
- Loyalty
- Respectfulness
- Responsibility

- Humility
- Compassion
- Fairness
- Forgiveness
- Authenticity

Gratitude is key and visualizing in the present moment, exactly what you hold in your mind's eye, take 2 minutes to visualize your board members, in the present tense and feel it in you heart as if the goal is already complete.

TOP THREE THINGS YOU ARE GREATFUL FOR:

1. _____
2. _____
3. _____

FOCUS ON YOUR ONE THING TODAY & TAKE MASSIVE ACTION!

"Self-confidence is the memory of success."

—DAVID STOREY

———————

Here are the Traits of the GREATS required to choose your superstar board members:

- Integrity
- Honesty
- Loyalty
- Respectfulness
- Responsibility

- Humility
- Compassion
- Fairness
- Forgiveness
- Authenticity

Gratitude is key and visualizing in the present moment, exactly what you hold in your mind's eye, take 2 minutes to visualize your board members, in the present tense and feel it in you heart as if the goal is already complete.

TOP THREE THINGS YOU ARE GREATFUL FOR:

1. _____
2. _____
3. _____

FOCUS ON YOUR ONE THING TODAY & TAKE MASSIVE ACTION!

"Without self-confidence, we are as babes in the cradle."

—VIRGINIA WOOLF

———————

Here are the Traits of the GREATS required to choose your superstar board members:

- Integrity
- Honesty
- Loyalty
- Respectfulness
- Responsibility

- Humility
- Compassion
- Fairness
- Forgiveness
- Authenticity

Gratitude is key and visualizing in the present moment, exactly what you hold in your mind's eye, take 2 minutes to visualize your board members, in the present tense and feel it in you heart as if the goal is already complete.

TOP THREE THINGS YOU ARE GREATFUL FOR:

1. _____
2. _____
3. _____

FOCUS ON YOUR ONE THING TODAY & TAKE MASSIVE ACTION!

*"Success is not final, failure is not fatal: it is the
courage to continue that counts."*

—WINSTON CHURCHILL

Here are the Traits of the GREATS required to choose your superstar board members:

- Integrity
- Honesty
- Loyalty
- Respectfulness
- Responsibility

- Humility
- Compassion
- Fairness
- Forgiveness
- Authenticity

Gratitude is key and visualizing in the present moment, exactly what you hold in your mind's eye, take 2 minutes to visualize your board members, in the present tense and feel it in you heart as if the goal is already complete.

TOP THREE THINGS YOU ARE GREATFUL FOR:

1. _____
2. _____
3. _____

FOCUS ON YOUR ONE THING TODAY & TAKE MASSIVE ACTION!

"Courage is the most important of all the virtues because, without courage, you can't practice any other virtue consistently."

—MAYA ANGELOU

———————

Here are the Traits of the GREATS required to choose your superstar board members:

- Integrity
- Honesty
- Loyalty
- Respectfulness
- Responsibility

- Humility
- Compassion
- Fairness
- Forgiveness
- Authenticity

Gratitude is key and visualizing in the present moment, exactly what you hold in your mind's eye, take 2 minutes to visualize your board members, in the present tense and feel it in you heart as if the goal is already complete.

TOP THREE THINGS YOU ARE GREATFUL FOR:

1. _____
2. _____
3. _____

FOCUS ON YOUR ONE THING TODAY & TAKE MASSIVE ACTION!

"Courage is resistance to fear, mastery
of fear—not absence of fear."

—MARK TWAIN

———————

Here are the Traits of the GREATS required to choose your superstar board members:

- Integrity
- Honesty
- Loyalty
- Respectfulness
- Responsibility

- Humility
- Compassion
- Fairness
- Forgiveness
- Authenticity

Gratitude is key and visualizing in the present moment, exactly what you hold in your mind's eye, take 2 minutes to visualize your board members, in the present tense and feel it in you heart as if the goal is already complete.

TOP THREE THINGS YOU ARE GREATFUL FOR:

1. _____

2. _____

3. _____

FOCUS ON YOUR ONE THING TODAY & TAKE MASSIVE ACTION!

"Failures are made only by those who fail to dare, not by those who dare to fail."

—LESTER B. PEARSON

———————

Here are the Traits of the GREATS required to choose your superstar board members:

- Integrity
- Honesty
- Loyalty
- Respectfulness
- Responsibility

- Humility
- Compassion
- Fairness
- Forgiveness
- Authenticity

Gratitude is key and visualizing in the present moment, exactly what you hold in your mind's eye, take 2 minutes to visualize your board members, in the present tense and feel it in you heart as if the goal is already complete.

TOP THREE THINGS YOU ARE GREATFUL FOR:

1. _____
2. _____
3. _____

FOCUS ON YOUR ONE THING TODAY & TAKE MASSIVE ACTION!

"Far better is it to dare mighty things, to win glorious triumphs even though checkered by failure than to take rank with those poor spirits who neither enjoy much nor suffer much because they live in the grey twilight that knows neither victory nor defeat."

—THEODORE ROOSEVELT

———————

Here are the Traits of the GREATS required to choose your superstar board members:

- Integrity
- Honesty
- Loyalty
- Respectfulness
- Responsibility

- Humility
- Compassion
- Fairness
- Forgiveness
- Authenticity

Gratitude is key and visualizing in the present moment, exactly what you hold in your mind's eye, take 2 minutes to visualize your board members, in the present tense and feel it in you heart as if the goal is already complete.

TOP THREE THINGS YOU ARE GREATFUL FOR:

1. _____
2. _____
3. _____

FOCUS ON YOUR ONE THING TODAY & TAKE MASSIVE ACTION!

"Dare to dream, but even more importantly, dare to put action behind your dreams."

—JOSH HINDS

———————

Here are the Traits of the GREATS required to choose your superstar board members:

- Integrity
- Honesty
- Loyalty
- Respectfulness
- Responsibility

- Humility
- Compassion
- Fairness
- Forgiveness
- Authenticity

Gratitude is key and visualizing in the present moment, exactly what you hold in your mind's eye, take 2 minutes to visualize your board members, in the present tense and feel it in you heart as if the goal is already complete.

TOP THREE THINGS YOU ARE GREATFUL FOR:

1. _____
2. _____
3. _____

FOCUS ON YOUR ONE THING TODAY & TAKE MASSIVE ACTION!

*"Failure will never overtake me if my determination
to succeed is strong enough."*

—OG MANDINO

———————

Here are the Traits of the GREATS required to choose your superstar board members:

- Integrity
- Honesty
- Loyalty
- Respectfulness
- Responsibility

- Humility
- Compassion
- Fairness
- Forgiveness
- Authenticity

Gratitude is key and visualizing in the present moment, exactly what you hold in your mind's eye, take 2 minutes to visualize your board members, in the present tense and feel it in you heart as if the goal is already complete.

TOP THREE THINGS YOU ARE GREATFUL FOR:

1. _____
2. _____
3. _____

FOCUS ON YOUR ONE THING TODAY & TAKE MASSIVE ACTION!

"A vow is fixed and unalterable determination to do a thing when such a determination is related to something noble which can only uplift the man who makes the resolve."

—MAHATMA GANDHI

———————

Here are the Traits of the GREATS required to choose your superstar board members:

- Integrity
- Honesty
- Loyalty
- Respectfulness
- Responsibility

- Humility
- Compassion
- Fairness
- Forgiveness
- Authenticity

Gratitude is key and visualizing in the present moment, exactly what you hold in your mind's eye, take 2 minutes to visualize your board members, in the present tense and feel it in you heart as if the goal is already complete.

TOP THREE THINGS YOU ARE GREATFUL FOR:

1. _____
2. _____
3. _____

FOCUS ON YOUR ONE THING TODAY & TAKE MASSIVE ACTION!

"Desire is the key to motivation, but it's the determination and commitment to an unrelenting pursuit of your goal—a commitment to excellence—that will enable you to attain the success you seek."

—MARIO ANDRETTI

———————

Here are the Traits of the GREATS required to choose your superstar board members:

- Integrity
- Honesty
- Loyalty
- Respectfulness
- Responsibility

- Humility
- Compassion
- Fairness
- Forgiveness
- Authenticity

Gratitude is key and visualizing in the present moment, exactly what you hold in your mind's eye, take 2 minutes to visualize your board members, in the present tense and feel it in you heart as if the goal is already complete.

TOP THREE THINGS YOU ARE GREATFUL FOR:

1. _____
2. _____
3. _____

FOCUS ON YOUR ONE THING TODAY & TAKE MASSIVE ACTION!

*"You can do anything as long as you have the passion,
the drive, the focus, and the support."*

—SABRINA BRYAN

———————

Here are the Traits of the GREATS required to choose your superstar board members:

- Integrity
- Honesty
- Loyalty
- Respectfulness
- Responsibility

- Humility
- Compassion
- Fairness
- Forgiveness
- Authenticity

Gratitude is key and visualizing in the present moment, exactly what you hold in your mind's eye, take 2 minutes to visualize your board members, in the present tense and feel it in you heart as if the goal is already complete.

TOP THREE THINGS YOU ARE GREATFUL FOR:

1. _____
2. _____
3. _____

FOCUS ON YOUR ONE THING TODAY & TAKE MASSIVE ACTION!

"The road to success is not easy to navigate, but with hard work, drive, and passion, it's possible to achieve the American dream."

—TOMMY HILFIGER

Here are the Traits of the GREATS required to choose your superstar board members:

- Integrity
- Honesty
- Loyalty
- Respectfulness
- Responsibility

- Humility
- Compassion
- Fairness
- Forgiveness
- Authenticity

Gratitude is key and visualizing in the present moment, exactly what you hold in your mind's eye, take 2 minutes to visualize your board members, in the present tense and feel it in you heart as if the goal is already complete.

TOP THREE THINGS YOU ARE GREATFUL FOR:

1. _____
2. _____
3. _____

FOCUS ON YOUR ONE THING TODAY & TAKE MASSIVE ACTION!

"Good business leaders create a vision, articulate the vision, passionately own the vision, and relentlessly drive it to completion."

—JACK WELCH

———————

Here are the Traits of the GREATS required to choose your superstar board members:

- Integrity
- Honesty
- Loyalty
- Respectfulness
- Responsibility

- Humility
- Compassion
- Fairness
- Forgiveness
- Authenticity

Gratitude is key and visualizing in the present moment, exactly what you hold in your mind's eye, take 2 minutes to visualize your board members, in the present tense and feel it in you heart as if the goal is already complete.

TOP THREE THINGS YOU ARE GREATFUL FOR:

1. _____
2. _____
3. _____

FOCUS ON YOUR ONE THING TODAY & TAKE MASSIVE ACTION!

"The mind is the limit. As long as the mind can envision the fact that you can do something, you can do it, as long as you really believe 100 percent."

—ARNOLD SCHWARZENEGGER

———————

Here are the Traits of the GREATS required to choose your superstar board members:

- Integrity
- Honesty
- Loyalty
- Respectfulness
- Responsibility

- Humility
- Compassion
- Fairness
- Forgiveness
- Authenticity

Gratitude is key and visualizing in the present moment, exactly what you hold in your mind's eye, take 2 minutes to visualize your board members, in the present tense and feel it in you heart as if the goal is already complete.

TOP THREE THINGS YOU ARE GREATFUL FOR:

1. _____
2. _____
3. _____

FOCUS ON YOUR ONE THING TODAY & TAKE MASSIVE ACTION!

"Envisioning the end is enough to put the means in motion."

—DORTHEA BRANDE

Here are the Traits of the GREATS required to choose your superstar board members:

- Integrity
- Honesty
- Loyalty
- Respectfulness
- Responsibility

- Humility
- Compassion
- Fairness
- Forgiveness
- Authenticity

Gratitude is key and visualizing in the present moment, exactly what you hold in your mind's eye, take 2 minutes to visualize your board members, in the present tense and feel it in you heart as if the goal is already complete.

TOP THREE THINGS YOU ARE GREATFUL FOR:

1. _____
2. _____
3. _____

FOCUS ON YOUR ONE THING TODAY & TAKE MASSIVE ACTION!

*"I am an artist, and I have the ability and the free will
to choose the way the world will envision me."*

—LADY GAGA

Here are the Traits of the GREATS required to choose your superstar board members:

- Integrity
- Honesty
- Loyalty
- Respectfulness
- Responsibility

- Humility
- Compassion
- Fairness
- Forgiveness
- Authenticity

Gratitude is key and visualizing in the present moment, exactly what you hold in your mind's eye, take 2 minutes to visualize your board members, in the present tense and feel it in you heart as if the goal is already complete.

TOP THREE THINGS YOU ARE GREATFUL FOR:

1. _____
2. _____
3. _____

FOCUS ON YOUR ONE THING TODAY & TAKE MASSIVE ACTION!

"Excellence is not a skill, it's an attitude."

—RALPH MARSTON

———————————

Here are the Traits of the GREATS required to choose your superstar board members:

- Integrity
- Honesty
- Loyalty
- Respectfulness
- Responsibility

- Humility
- Compassion
- Fairness
- Forgiveness
- Authenticity

Gratitude is key and visualizing in the present moment, exactly what you hold in your mind's eye, take 2 minutes to visualize your board members, in the present tense and feel it in you heart as if the goal is already complete.

TOP THREE THINGS YOU ARE GREATFUL FOR:

1. _____
2. _____
3. _____

FOCUS ON YOUR ONE THING TODAY & TAKE MASSIVE ACTION!

"We are what we repeatedly do. Excellence,
therefore, is not an act, but a habit."

—ARISTOTLE

———————

Here are the Traits of the GREATS required to choose your superstar board members:

- Integrity
- Honesty
- Loyalty
- Respectfulness
- Responsibility

- Humility
- Compassion
- Fairness
- Forgiveness
- Authenticity

Gratitude is key and visualizing in the present moment, exactly what you hold in your mind's eye, take 2 minutes to visualize your board members, in the present tense and feel it in you heart as if the goal is already complete.

TOP THREE THINGS YOU ARE GREATFUL FOR:

1. _____
2. _____
3. _____

FOCUS ON YOUR ONE THING TODAY & TAKE MASSIVE ACTION!

"Excellence is a continuous process and not an accident."

—ABDUL KALAM

———————————

Here are the Traits of the GREATS required to choose your superstar board members:

- Integrity
- Honesty
- Loyalty
- Respectfulness
- Responsibility

- Humility
- Compassion
- Fairness
- Forgiveness
- Authenticity

Gratitude is key and visualizing in the present moment, exactly what you hold in your mind's eye, take 2 minutes to visualize your board members, in the present tense and feel it in you heart as if the goal is already complete.

TOP THREE THINGS YOU ARE GREATFUL FOR:

1. _____
2. _____
3. _____

FOCUS ON YOUR ONE THING TODAY & TAKE MASSIVE ACTION!

*"It is during our darkest moments
that we must focus to see the light."*

—ARISTOTLE

———————

Here are the Traits of the GREATS required to choose your superstar board members:

- Integrity
- Honesty
- Loyalty
- Respectfulness
- Responsibility

- Humility
- Compassion
- Fairness
- Forgiveness
- Authenticity

Gratitude is key and visualizing in the present moment, exactly what you hold in your mind's eye, take 2 minutes to visualize your board members, in the present tense and feel it in you heart as if the goal is already complete.

TOP THREE THINGS YOU ARE GREATFUL FOR:

1. _____
2. _____
3. _____

FOCUS ON YOUR ONE THING TODAY & TAKE MASSIVE ACTION!

"I don't care how much power, brilliance or energy you have, if you don't harness it and focus it on a specific target, and hold it there you're never going to accomplish as much as your ability warrants."

—ZIG ZIGLAR

———————

Here are the Traits of the GREATS required to choose your superstar board members:

- Integrity
- Honesty
- Loyalty
- Respectfulness
- Responsibility

- Humility
- Compassion
- Fairness
- Forgiveness
- Authenticity

Gratitude is key and visualizing in the present moment, exactly what you hold in your mind's eye, take 2 minutes to visualize your board members, in the present tense and feel it in you heart as if the goal is already complete.

TOP THREE THINGS YOU ARE GREATFUL FOR:

1. _____
2. _____
3. _____

FOCUS ON YOUR ONE THING TODAY & TAKE MASSIVE ACTION!

*"Your destiny is to fulfill those things upon which you focus most intently.
So choose to keep your focus on that which is truly magnificent, beautiful,
uplifting and joyful. Your life is always moving toward something."*

—RALPH MARSTON

———————————

Here are the Traits of the GREATS required to choose your superstar board members:

- Integrity
- Honesty
- Loyalty
- Respectfulness
- Responsibility

- Humility
- Compassion
- Fairness
- Forgiveness
- Authenticity

Gratitude is key and visualizing in the present moment, exactly what you hold in your mind's eye, take 2 minutes to visualize your board members, in the present tense and feel it in you heart as if the goal is already complete.

TOP THREE THINGS YOU ARE GREATFUL FOR:

1. _____
2. _____
3. _____

FOCUS ON YOUR ONE THING TODAY & TAKE MASSIVE ACTION!

"Forgiveness doesn't make the other person right; it makes you free."

—STORMIE OMARTIAN

———————

Here are the Traits of the GREATS required to choose your superstar board members:

- Integrity
- Honesty
- Loyalty
- Respectfulness
- Responsibility

- Humility
- Compassion
- Fairness
- Forgiveness
- Authenticity

Gratitude is key and visualizing in the present moment, exactly what you hold in your mind's eye, take 2 minutes to visualize your board members, in the present tense and feel it in you heart as if the goal is already complete.

TOP THREE THINGS YOU ARE GREATFUL FOR:

1. _____
2. _____
3. _____

FOCUS ON YOUR ONE THING TODAY & TAKE MASSIVE ACTION!

"Forgiveness is the fragrance that the violet
sheds on the heel that has crushed it."

—MARK TWAIN

Here are the Traits of the GREATS required to choose your superstar board members:

- Integrity
- Honesty
- Loyalty
- Respectfulness
- Responsibility

- Humility
- Compassion
- Fairness
- Forgiveness
- Authenticity

Gratitude is key and visualizing in the present moment, exactly what you hold in your mind's eye, take 2 minutes to visualize your board members, in the present tense and feel it in you heart as if the goal is already complete.

TOP THREE THINGS YOU ARE GREATFUL FOR:

1. _____
2. _____
3. _____

FOCUS ON YOUR ONE THING TODAY & TAKE MASSIVE ACTION!

"The weak can never forgive. Forgiveness is the attribute of the strong."

—MAHATMA GANDHI

———————

Here are the Traits of the GREATS required to choose your superstar board members:

- Integrity
- Honesty
- Loyalty
- Respectfulness
- Responsibility

- Humility
- Compassion
- Fairness
- Forgiveness
- Authenticity

Gratitude is key and visualizing in the present moment, exactly what you hold in your mind's eye, take 2 minutes to visualize your board members, in the present tense and feel it in you heart as if the goal is already complete.

TOP THREE THINGS YOU ARE GREATFUL FOR:

1. _____
2. _____
3. _____

FOCUS ON YOUR ONE THING TODAY & TAKE MASSIVE ACTION!

"Only those who have learned the power of sincere and selfless contribution experience life's deepest joy: true fulfillment."

—TONY ROBBINS

———————

Here are the Traits of the GREATS required to choose your superstar board members:

- Integrity
- Honesty
- Loyalty
- Respectfulness
- Responsibility

- Humility
- Compassion
- Fairness
- Forgiveness
- Authenticity

Gratitude is key and visualizing in the present moment, exactly what you hold in your mind's eye, take 2 minutes to visualize your board members, in the present tense and feel it in you heart as if the goal is already complete.

TOP THREE THINGS YOU ARE GREATFUL FOR:

1. _____
2. _____
3. _____

FOCUS ON YOUR ONE THING TODAY & TAKE MASSIVE ACTION!

"If you devote yourself entirely to a noble pursuit, there is no way you cannot find beauty and fulfillment."

—DANIEL GILLIES

Here are the Traits of the GREATS required to choose your superstar board members:

- Integrity
- Honesty
- Loyalty
- Respectfulness
- Responsibility

- Humility
- Compassion
- Fairness
- Forgiveness
- Authenticity

Gratitude is key and visualizing in the present moment, exactly what you hold in your mind's eye, take 2 minutes to visualize your board members, in the present tense and feel it in you heart as if the goal is already complete.

TOP THREE THINGS YOU ARE GREATFUL FOR:

1. _____
2. _____
3. _____

FOCUS ON YOUR ONE THING TODAY & TAKE MASSIVE ACTION!

"True happiness is a state of fulfillment."

—ASHISH SOPHAT

———————

Here are the Traits of the GREATS required to choose your superstar board members:

- Integrity
- Honesty
- Loyalty
- Respectfulness
- Responsibility

- Humility
- Compassion
- Fairness
- Forgiveness
- Authenticity

Gratitude is key and visualizing in the present moment, exactly what you hold in your mind's eye, take 2 minutes to visualize your board members, in the present tense and feel it in you heart as if the goal is already complete.

TOP THREE THINGS YOU ARE GREATFUL FOR:

1. _____
2. _____
3. _____

FOCUS ON YOUR ONE THING TODAY & TAKE MASSIVE ACTION!

"Set your goals high, and don't stop 'til you get there."

—BO JACKSON

———————

Here are the Traits of the GREATS required to choose your superstar board members:

- Integrity
- Honesty
- Loyalty
- Respectfulness
- Responsibility

- Humility
- Compassion
- Fairness
- Forgiveness
- Authenticity

Gratitude is key and visualizing in the present moment, exactly what you hold in your mind's eye, take 2 minutes to visualize your board members, in the present tense and feel it in you heart as if the goal is already complete.

TOP THREE THINGS YOU ARE GREATFUL FOR:

1. _____
2. _____
3. _____

FOCUS ON YOUR ONE THING TODAY & TAKE MASSIVE ACTION!

"Goals. There's no telling what you can do when you get inspired by them. There's no telling what you can do when you believe in them. And there's no telling what will happen when you act upon them."

—JIM ROHN

———————

Here are the Traits of the GREATS required to choose your superstar board members:

- Integrity
- Honesty
- Loyalty
- Respectfulness
- Responsibility

- Humility
- Compassion
- Fairness
- Forgiveness
- Authenticity

Gratitude is key and visualizing in the present moment, exactly what you hold in your mind's eye, take 2 minutes to visualize your board members, in the present tense and feel it in you heart as if the goal is already complete.

TOP THREE THINGS YOU ARE GREATFUL FOR:

1. _____
2. _____
3. _____

FOCUS ON YOUR ONE THING TODAY & TAKE MASSIVE ACTION!

"If you set goals and go after them with all the determination you can muster, your gifts will take you places that will amaze you."

—LES BROWN

Here are the Traits of the GREATS required to choose your superstar board members:

- Integrity
- Honesty
- Loyalty
- Respectfulness
- Responsibility

- Humility
- Compassion
- Fairness
- Forgiveness
- Authenticity

Gratitude is key and visualizing in the present moment, exactly what you hold in your mind's eye, take 2 minutes to visualize your board members, in the present tense and feel it in you heart as if the goal is already complete.

TOP THREE THINGS YOU ARE GREATFUL FOR:

1. _____
2. _____
3. _____

FOCUS ON YOUR ONE THING TODAY & TAKE MASSIVE ACTION!

"Thankfulness is the beginning of gratitude. Gratitude is the completion of thankfulness. Thankfulness may consist merely of words. Gratitude is shown in acts."

—HENRI FREDERIC AMIEL

Here are the Traits of the GREATS required to choose your superstar board members:

- Integrity
- Honesty
- Loyalty
- Respectfulness
- Responsibility

- Humility
- Compassion
- Fairness
- Forgiveness
- Authenticity

Gratitude is key and visualizing in the present moment, exactly what you hold in your mind's eye, take 2 minutes to visualize your board members, in the present tense and feel it in you heart as if the goal is already complete.

TOP THREE THINGS YOU ARE GREATFUL FOR:

1. _____
2. _____
3. _____

FOCUS ON YOUR ONE THING TODAY & TAKE MASSIVE ACTION!

*"I would maintain that thanks are the highest form of thought
and that gratitude is happiness doubled by wonder."*

—GILBERT K. CHESTERTON

———————————

Here are the Traits of the GREATS required to choose your superstar board members:

- Integrity
- Honesty
- Loyalty
- Respectfulness
- Responsibility

- Humility
- Compassion
- Fairness
- Forgiveness
- Authenticity

Gratitude is key and visualizing in the present moment, exactly what you hold in your mind's eye, take 2 minutes to visualize your board members, in the present tense and feel it in you heart as if the goal is already complete.

TOP THREE THINGS YOU ARE GREATFUL FOR:

1. _____
2. _____
3. _____

FOCUS ON YOUR ONE THING TODAY & TAKE MASSIVE ACTION!

"Gratitude is the healthiest of all human emotions. The more you express gratitude for what you have, the more likely you will have even more to express gratitude for."

—ZIG ZIGLAR

———

Here are the Traits of the GREATS required to choose your superstar board members:

- Integrity
- Honesty
- Loyalty
- Respectfulness
- Responsibility

- Humility
- Compassion
- Fairness
- Forgiveness
- Authenticity

Gratitude is key and visualizing in the present moment, exactly what you hold in your mind's eye, take 2 minutes to visualize your board members, in the present tense and feel it in you heart as if the goal is already complete.

TOP THREE THINGS YOU ARE GREATFUL FOR:

1. _____
2. _____
3. _____

FOCUS ON YOUR ONE THING TODAY & TAKE MASSIVE ACTION!

"Honesty is the first chapter in the book of wisdom."

—THOMAS JEFFERSON

———————

Here are the Traits of the GREATS required to choose your superstar board members:

- Integrity
- Honesty
- Loyalty
- Respectfulness
- Responsibility

- Humility
- Compassion
- Fairness
- Forgiveness
- Authenticity

Gratitude is key and visualizing in the present moment, exactly what you hold in your mind's eye, take 2 minutes to visualize your board members, in the present tense and feel it in you heart as if the goal is already complete.

TOP THREE THINGS YOU ARE GREATFUL FOR:

1. _____
2. _____
3. _____

FOCUS ON YOUR ONE THING TODAY & TAKE MASSIVE ACTION!

*"Being honest may not get you a lot of friends but
it'll always get you the right ones."*

—JOHN LENNON

———————

Here are the Traits of the GREATS required to choose your superstar board members:

- Integrity
- Honesty
- Loyalty
- Respectfulness
- Responsibility

- Humility
- Compassion
- Fairness
- Forgiveness
- Authenticity

Gratitude is key and visualizing in the present moment, exactly what you hold in your mind's eye, take 2 minutes to visualize your board members, in the present tense and feel it in you heart as if the goal is already complete.

TOP THREE THINGS YOU ARE GREATFUL FOR:

1. _____
2. _____
3. _____

FOCUS ON YOUR ONE THING TODAY & TAKE MASSIVE ACTION!

"Honesty and transparency make you vulnerable.
Be honest and transparent anyway."

—MOTHER

———————

Here are the Traits of the GREATS required to choose your superstar board members:

- Integrity
- Honesty
- Loyalty
- Respectfulness
- Responsibility

- Humility
- Compassion
- Fairness
- Forgiveness
- Authenticity

Gratitude is key and visualizing in the present moment, exactly what you hold in your mind's eye, take 2 minutes to visualize your board members, in the present tense and feel it in you heart as if the goal is already complete.

TOP THREE THINGS YOU ARE GREATFUL FOR:

1. _____
2. _____
3. _____

FOCUS ON YOUR ONE THING TODAY & TAKE MASSIVE ACTION!

*"Hope is being able to see that there
is light despite all of the darkness."*

—DESMOND TUTU

———————

Here are the Traits of the GREATS required to choose your superstar board members:

- Integrity
- Honesty
- Loyalty
- Respectfulness
- Responsibility

- Humility
- Compassion
- Fairness
- Forgiveness
- Authenticity

Gratitude is key and visualizing in the present moment, exactly what you hold in your mind's eye, take 2 minutes to visualize your board members, in the present tense and feel it in you heart as if the goal is already complete.

TOP THREE THINGS YOU ARE GREATFUL FOR:

1. _____
2. _____
3. _____

FOCUS ON YOUR ONE THING TODAY & TAKE MASSIVE ACTION!

*"We must accept finite disappointment
but never lose infinite hope."*

—MARTIN LUTHER KING, JR.

———————

Here are the Traits of the GREATS required to choose your superstar board members:

- Integrity
- Honesty
- Loyalty
- Respectfulness
- Responsibility

- Humility
- Compassion
- Fairness
- Forgiveness
- Authenticity

Gratitude is key and visualizing in the present moment, exactly what you hold in your mind's eye, take 2 minutes to visualize your board members, in the present tense and feel it in you heart as if the goal is already complete.

TOP THREE THINGS YOU ARE GREATFUL FOR:

1. _____
2. _____
3. _____

FOCUS ON YOUR ONE THING TODAY & TAKE MASSIVE ACTION!

*"What oxygen is to the lungs, such
is hope to the meaning of life."*

—EMIL BRUNNER

———————

Here are the Traits of the GREATS required to choose your superstar board members:

- Integrity
- Honesty
- Loyalty
- Respectfulness
- Responsibility

- Humility
- Compassion
- Fairness
- Forgiveness
- Authenticity

Gratitude is key and visualizing in the present moment, exactly what you hold in your mind's eye, take 2 minutes to visualize your board members, in the present tense and feel it in you heart as if the goal is already complete.

TOP THREE THINGS YOU ARE GREATFUL FOR:

1. _____

2. _____

3. _____

FOCUS ON YOUR ONE THING TODAY & TAKE MASSIVE ACTION!

"The true sign of intelligence is not knowledge but imagination."

—ALBERT EINSTEIN

———————

Here are the Traits of the GREATS required to choose your superstar board members:

- Integrity
- Honesty
- Loyalty
- Respectfulness
- Responsibility

- Humility
- Compassion
- Fairness
- Forgiveness
- Authenticity

Gratitude is key and visualizing in the present moment, exactly what you hold in your mind's eye, take 2 minutes to visualize your board members, in the present tense and feel it in you heart as if the goal is already complete.

TOP THREE THINGS YOU ARE GREATFUL FOR:

1. _____
2. _____
3. _____

FOCUS ON YOUR ONE THING TODAY & TAKE MASSIVE ACTION!

"Imagination will often carry us to worlds that never were. But without it, we go nowhere."

—CARL SAGAN

———————

Here are the Traits of the GREATS required to choose your superstar board members:

- Integrity
- Honesty
- Loyalty
- Respectfulness
- Responsibility

- Humility
- Compassion
- Fairness
- Forgiveness
- Authenticity

Gratitude is key and visualizing in the present moment, exactly what you hold in your mind's eye, take 2 minutes to visualize your board members, in the present tense and feel it in you heart as if the goal is already complete.

TOP THREE THINGS YOU ARE GREATFUL FOR:

1. _____
2. _____
3. _____

FOCUS ON YOUR ONE THING TODAY & TAKE MASSIVE ACTION!

*"Laughter is timeless, imagination has
no age and dreams are forever."*

—WALT DISNEY

———————

Here are the Traits of the GREATS required to choose your superstar board members:

- Integrity
- Honesty
- Loyalty
- Respectfulness
- Responsibility

- Humility
- Compassion
- Fairness
- Forgiveness
- Authenticity

Gratitude is key and visualizing in the present moment, exactly what you hold in your mind's eye, take 2 minutes to visualize your board members, in the present tense and feel it in you heart as if the goal is already complete.

TOP THREE THINGS YOU ARE GREATFUL FOR:

1. _____
2. _____
3. _____

FOCUS ON YOUR ONE THING TODAY & TAKE MASSIVE ACTION!

"What you do today can improve all your tomorrows."

—RALPH MARSTON

Here are the Traits of the GREATS required to choose your superstar board members:

- Integrity
- Honesty
- Loyalty
- Respectfulness
- Responsibility

- Humility
- Compassion
- Fairness
- Forgiveness
- Authenticity

Gratitude is key and visualizing in the present moment, exactly what you hold in your mind's eye, take 2 minutes to visualize your board members, in the present tense and feel it in you heart as if the goal is already complete.

TOP THREE THINGS YOU ARE GREATFUL FOR:

1. _____
2. _____
3. _____

FOCUS ON YOUR ONE THING TODAY & TAKE MASSIVE ACTION!

"There is nothing noble in being superior to your fellow man; true nobility is being superior to your former self."

—ERNEST HEMINGWAY

———————

Here are the Traits of the GREATS required to choose your superstar board members:

- Integrity
- Honesty
- Loyalty
- Respectfulness
- Responsibility

- Humility
- Compassion
- Fairness
- Forgiveness
- Authenticity

Gratitude is key and visualizing in the present moment, exactly what you hold in your mind's eye, take 2 minutes to visualize your board members, in the present tense and feel it in you heart as if the goal is already complete.

TOP THREE THINGS YOU ARE GREATFUL FOR:

1. _____
2. _____
3. _____

FOCUS ON YOUR ONE THING TODAY & TAKE MASSIVE ACTION!

*"Become addicted to constant and
never-ending self-improvement."*

—ANTHONY J. D'ANGELO

———————

Here are the Traits of the GREATS required to choose your superstar board members:

- Integrity
- Honesty
- Loyalty
- Respectfulness
- Responsibility

- Humility
- Compassion
- Fairness
- Forgiveness
- Authenticity

Gratitude is key and visualizing in the present moment, exactly what you hold in your mind's eye, take 2 minutes to visualize your board members, in the present tense and feel it in you heart as if the goal is already complete.

TOP THREE THINGS YOU ARE GREATFUL FOR:

1. _____
2. _____
3. _____

FOCUS ON YOUR ONE THING TODAY & TAKE MASSIVE ACTION!

*"Genius is one percent inspiration and
ninety-nine percent perspiration."*

—THOMAS A. EDISON

———————

Here are the Traits of the GREATS required to choose your superstar board members:

- Integrity
- Honesty
- Loyalty
- Respectfulness
- Responsibility

- Humility
- Compassion
- Fairness
- Forgiveness
- Authenticity

Gratitude is key and visualizing in the present moment, exactly what you hold in your mind's eye, take 2 minutes to visualize your board members, in the present tense and feel it in you heart as if the goal is already complete.

TOP THREE THINGS YOU ARE GREATFUL FOR:

1. _____
2. _____
3. _____

FOCUS ON YOUR ONE THING TODAY & TAKE MASSIVE ACTION!

"Inspiration comes from within yourself. One has to be positive. When you're positive, good things happen."

—DEEP ROY

———————

Here are the Traits of the GREATS required to choose your superstar board members:

- Integrity
- Honesty
- Loyalty
- Respectfulness
- Responsibility

- Humility
- Compassion
- Fairness
- Forgiveness
- Authenticity

Gratitude is key and visualizing in the present moment, exactly what you hold in your mind's eye, take 2 minutes to visualize your board members, in the present tense and feel it in you heart as if the goal is already complete.

TOP THREE THINGS YOU ARE GREATFUL FOR:

1. _____

2. _____

3. _____

FOCUS ON YOUR ONE THING TODAY & TAKE MASSIVE ACTION!

"You can't wait for inspiration. You have to go after it with a club."

—JACK LONDON

———————

Here are the Traits of the GREATS required to choose your superstar board members:

- Integrity
- Honesty
- Loyalty
- Respectfulness
- Responsibility

- Humility
- Compassion
- Fairness
- Forgiveness
- Authenticity

Gratitude is key and visualizing in the present moment, exactly what you hold in your mind's eye, take 2 minutes to visualize your board members, in the present tense and feel it in you heart as if the goal is already complete.

TOP THREE THINGS YOU ARE GREATFUL FOR:

1. _____
2. _____
3. _____

FOCUS ON YOUR ONE THING TODAY & TAKE MASSIVE ACTION!

"Happiness lies in the joy of achievement
and the thrill of creative effort."

—FRANKLIN D. ROOSEVELT

———————

Here are the Traits of the GREATS required to choose your superstar board members:

- Integrity
- Honesty
- Loyalty
- Respectfulness
- Responsibility

- Humility
- Compassion
- Fairness
- Forgiveness
- Authenticity

Gratitude is key and visualizing in the present moment, exactly what you hold in your mind's eye, take 2 minutes to visualize your board members, in the present tense and feel it in you heart as if the goal is already complete.

TOP THREE THINGS YOU ARE GREATFUL FOR:

1. _____
2. _____
3. _____

FOCUS ON YOUR ONE THING TODAY & TAKE MASSIVE ACTION!

*"We cannot cure the world of sorrows,
but we can choose to live in joy."*

—JOSEPH CAMPBELL

Here are the Traits of the GREATS required to choose your superstar board members:

- Integrity
- Honesty
- Loyalty
- Respectfulness
- Responsibility

- Humility
- Compassion
- Fairness
- Forgiveness
- Authenticity

Gratitude is key and visualizing in the present moment, exactly what you hold in your mind's eye, take 2 minutes to visualize your board members, in the present tense and feel it in you heart as if the goal is already complete.

TOP THREE THINGS YOU ARE GREATFUL FOR:

1. _____
2. _____
3. _____

FOCUS ON YOUR ONE THING TODAY & TAKE MASSIVE ACTION!

"The soul's joy lies in doing."

—PERCY BYSSHE SHELLEY

———————

Here are the Traits of the GREATS required to choose your superstar board members:

- Integrity
- Honesty
- Loyalty
- Respectfulness
- Responsibility

- Humility
- Compassion
- Fairness
- Forgiveness
- Authenticity

Gratitude is key and visualizing in the present moment, exactly what you hold in your mind's eye, take 2 minutes to visualize your board members, in the present tense and feel it in you heart as if the goal is already complete.

TOP THREE THINGS YOU ARE GREATFUL FOR:

1. _____
2. _____
3. _____

FOCUS ON YOUR ONE THING TODAY & TAKE MASSIVE ACTION!

"Kindness is the language which the deaf can hear and the blind can see."

—MARK TWAIN

———————

Here are the Traits of the GREATS required to choose your superstar board members:

- Integrity
- Honesty
- Loyalty
- Respectfulness
- Responsibility

- Humility
- Compassion
- Fairness
- Forgiveness
- Authenticity

Gratitude is key and visualizing in the present moment, exactly what you hold in your mind's eye, take 2 minutes to visualize your board members, in the present tense and feel it in you heart as if the goal is already complete.

TOP THREE THINGS YOU ARE GREATFUL FOR:

1. _____
2. _____
3. _____

FOCUS ON YOUR ONE THING TODAY & TAKE MASSIVE ACTION!

"One who knows how to show and to accept kindness will be a friend better than any possession."

—SOPHOCLES

———————

Here are the Traits of the GREATS required to choose your superstar board members:

- Integrity
- Honesty
- Loyalty
- Respectfulness
- Responsibility

- Humility
- Compassion
- Fairness
- Forgiveness
- Authenticity

Gratitude is key and visualizing in the present moment, exactly what you hold in your mind's eye, take 2 minutes to visualize your board members, in the present tense and feel it in you heart as if the goal is already complete.

TOP THREE THINGS YOU ARE GREATFUL FOR:

1. _____
2. _____
3. _____

FOCUS ON YOUR ONE THING TODAY & TAKE MASSIVE ACTION!

"There's no such thing as a small act of kindness. Every act creates a ripple with no logical end."

—SCOTT ADAMS

———————

Here are the Traits of the GREATS required to choose your superstar board members:

- Integrity
- Honesty
- Loyalty
- Respectfulness
- Responsibility

- Humility
- Compassion
- Fairness
- Forgiveness
- Authenticity

Gratitude is key and visualizing in the present moment, exactly what you hold in your mind's eye, take 2 minutes to visualize your board members, in the present tense and feel it in you heart as if the goal is already complete.

TOP THREE THINGS YOU ARE GREATFUL FOR:

1. _____
2. _____
3. _____

FOCUS ON YOUR ONE THING TODAY & TAKE MASSIVE ACTION!

"An investment in knowledge pays the best interest."

—BENJAMIN FRANKLIN

Here are the Traits of the GREATS required to choose your superstar board members:

- Integrity
- Honesty
- Loyalty
- Respectfulness
- Responsibility

- Humility
- Compassion
- Fairness
- Forgiveness
- Authenticity

Gratitude is key and visualizing in the present moment, exactly what you hold in your mind's eye, take 2 minutes to visualize your board members, in the present tense and feel it in you heart as if the goal is already complete.

TOP THREE THINGS YOU ARE GREATFUL FOR:

1. _____
2. _____
3. _____

FOCUS ON YOUR ONE THING TODAY & TAKE MASSIVE ACTION!

"Knowledge is power. Information is liberating. Education is the premise of progress, in every society, in every family."

—KOFI ANNAN

———————

Here are the Traits of the GREATS required to choose your superstar board members:

- Integrity
- Honesty
- Loyalty
- Respectfulness
- Responsibility

- Humility
- Compassion
- Fairness
- Forgiveness
- Authenticity

Gratitude is key and visualizing in the present moment, exactly what you hold in your mind's eye, take 2 minutes to visualize your board members, in the present tense and feel it in you heart as if the goal is already complete.

TOP THREE THINGS YOU ARE GREATFUL FOR:

1. _____
2. _____
3. _____

FOCUS ON YOUR ONE THING TODAY & TAKE MASSIVE ACTION!

"True friendship can afford true knowledge. It does not depend on darkness and ignorance."

—HENRY DAVID THOREAU

———————

Here are the Traits of the GREATS required to choose your superstar board members:

- Integrity
- Honesty
- Loyalty
- Respectfulness
- Responsibility

- Humility
- Compassion
- Fairness
- Forgiveness
- Authenticity

Gratitude is key and visualizing in the present moment, exactly what you hold in your mind's eye, take 2 minutes to visualize your board members, in the present tense and feel it in you heart as if the goal is already complete.

TOP THREE THINGS YOU ARE GREATFUL FOR:

1. _____
2. _____
3. _____

FOCUS ON YOUR ONE THING TODAY & TAKE MASSIVE ACTION!

"We have two ears and one mouth so that we can listen twice as much as we speak."

—EPICTETUS

———————

Here are the Traits of the GREATS required to choose your superstar board members:

- Integrity
- Honesty
- Loyalty
- Respectfulness
- Responsibility

- Humility
- Compassion
- Fairness
- Forgiveness
- Authenticity

Gratitude is key and visualizing in the present moment, exactly what you hold in your mind's eye, take 2 minutes to visualize your board members, in the present tense and feel it in you heart as if the goal is already complete.

TOP THREE THINGS YOU ARE GREATFUL FOR:

1. _____
2. _____
3. _____

FOCUS ON YOUR ONE THING TODAY & TAKE MASSIVE ACTION!

"Listen with the intent to understand, not the intent to reply."

—STEPHEN COVEY

———————

Here are the Traits of the GREATS required to choose your superstar board members:

- Integrity
- Honesty
- Loyalty
- Respectfulness
- Responsibility

- Humility
- Compassion
- Fairness
- Forgiveness
- Authenticity

Gratitude is key and visualizing in the present moment, exactly what you hold in your mind's eye, take 2 minutes to visualize your board members, in the present tense and feel it in you heart as if the goal is already complete.

TOP THREE THINGS YOU ARE GREATFUL FOR:

1. _____
2. _____
3. _____

FOCUS ON YOUR ONE THING TODAY & TAKE MASSIVE ACTION!

"There is only one role for being a good talker—learn to listen."

—CHRISTOPHER MORLEY

———————

Here are the Traits of the GREATS required to choose your superstar board members:

- Integrity
- Honesty
- Loyalty
- Respectfulness
- Responsibility

- Humility
- Compassion
- Fairness
- Forgiveness
- Authenticity

Gratitude is key and visualizing in the present moment, exactly what you hold in your mind's eye, take 2 minutes to visualize your board members, in the present tense and feel it in you heart as if the goal is already complete.

TOP THREE THINGS YOU ARE GREATFUL FOR:

1. _____
2. _____
3. _____

FOCUS ON YOUR ONE THING TODAY & TAKE MASSIVE ACTION!

"With mindfulness, you can establish yourself in the present in order to touch the wonders of life that are available in that moment."

—THICH NHAT HANH

———————

Here are the Traits of the GREATS required to choose your superstar board members:

- Integrity
- Honesty
- Loyalty
- Respectfulness
- Responsibility

- Humility
- Compassion
- Fairness
- Forgiveness
- Authenticity

Gratitude is key and visualizing in the present moment, exactly what you hold in your mind's eye, take 2 minutes to visualize your board members, in the present tense and feel it in you heart as if the goal is already complete.

TOP THREE THINGS YOU ARE GREATFUL FOR:

1. _____
2. _____
3. _____

FOCUS ON YOUR ONE THING TODAY & TAKE MASSIVE ACTION!

"Mindfulness helps you go home to the present. And every time you go there and recognize a condition of happiness that you have, happiness comes."

—THICH NHAT HANH

———————

Here are the Traits of the GREATS required to choose your superstar board members:

- Integrity
- Honesty
- Loyalty
- Respectfulness
- Responsibility

- Humility
- Compassion
- Fairness
- Forgiveness
- Authenticity

Gratitude is key and visualizing in the present moment, exactly what you hold in your mind's eye, take 2 minutes to visualize your board members, in the present tense and feel it in you heart as if the goal is already complete.

TOP THREE THINGS YOU ARE GREATFUL FOR:

1. _____
2. _____
3. _____

FOCUS ON YOUR ONE THING TODAY & TAKE MASSIVE ACTION!

"Mindfulness is about love and loving life. When you cultivate this love, it gives you clarity and compassion for life, and your actions happen in accordance with that."

—JON KABAT-ZINN

Here are the Traits of the GREATS required to choose your superstar board members:

- Integrity
- Honesty
- Loyalty
- Respectfulness
- Responsibility

- Humility
- Compassion
- Fairness
- Forgiveness
- Authenticity

Gratitude is key and visualizing in the present moment, exactly what you hold in your mind's eye, take 2 minutes to visualize your board members, in the present tense and feel it in you heart as if the goal is already complete.

TOP THREE THINGS YOU ARE GREATFUL FOR:

1. _____

2. _____

3. _____

FOCUS ON YOUR ONE THING TODAY & TAKE MASSIVE ACTION!

"To succeed in your mission, you must have single-minded devotion to your goal."

—A. P. J. ABDUL KALAM

Here are the Traits of the GREATS required to choose your superstar board members:

- Integrity
- Honesty
- Loyalty
- Respectfulness
- Responsibility

- Humility
- Compassion
- Fairness
- Forgiveness
- Authenticity

Gratitude is key and visualizing in the present moment, exactly what you hold in your mind's eye, take 2 minutes to visualize your board members, in the present tense and feel it in you heart as if the goal is already complete.

TOP THREE THINGS YOU ARE GREATFUL FOR:

1. _____
2. _____
3. _____

FOCUS ON YOUR ONE THING TODAY & TAKE MASSIVE ACTION!

"Outstanding people have one thing in common:
an absolute sense of mission."

—ZIG ZIGLAR

———————

Here are the Traits of the GREATS required to choose your superstar board members:

- Integrity
- Honesty
- Loyalty
- Respectfulness
- Responsibility

- Humility
- Compassion
- Fairness
- Forgiveness
- Authenticity

Gratitude is key and visualizing in the present moment, exactly what you hold in your mind's eye, take 2 minutes to visualize your board members, in the present tense and feel it in you heart as if the goal is already complete.

TOP THREE THINGS YOU ARE GREATFUL FOR:

1. _____
2. _____
3. _____

FOCUS ON YOUR ONE THING TODAY & TAKE MASSIVE ACTION!

"My measure of success is whether I'm fulfilling my mission."

—ROBERT KIYOSAKI

———————

Here are the Traits of the GREATS required to choose your superstar board members:

- Integrity
- Honesty
- Loyalty
- Respectfulness
- Responsibility

- Humility
- Compassion
- Fairness
- Forgiveness
- Authenticity

Gratitude is key and visualizing in the present moment, exactly what you hold in your mind's eye, take 2 minutes to visualize your board members, in the present tense and feel it in you heart as if the goal is already complete.

TOP THREE THINGS YOU ARE GREATFUL FOR:

1. _____
2. _____
3. _____

FOCUS ON YOUR ONE THING TODAY & TAKE MASSIVE ACTION!

"Nurture your mind with great thoughts. To believe in the heroic makes heroes."

—BENJAMIN DISRAELI

Here are the Traits of the GREATS required to choose your superstar board members:

- Integrity
- Honesty
- Loyalty
- Respectfulness
- Responsibility

- Humility
- Compassion
- Fairness
- Forgiveness
- Authenticity

Gratitude is key and visualizing in the present moment, exactly what you hold in your mind's eye, take 2 minutes to visualize your board members, in the present tense and feel it in you heart as if the goal is already complete.

TOP THREE THINGS YOU ARE GREATFUL FOR:

1. _____
2. _____
3. _____

FOCUS ON YOUR ONE THING TODAY & TAKE MASSIVE ACTION!

"The glory of gardening: hands in the dirt, head in the sun, heart with nature. To nurture a garden is to feed not just the body, but the soul."

—ALFRED AUSTIN

———————

Here are the Traits of the GREATS required to choose your superstar board members:

- Integrity
- Honesty
- Loyalty
- Respectfulness
- Responsibility

- Humility
- Compassion
- Fairness
- Forgiveness
- Authenticity

Gratitude is key and visualizing in the present moment, exactly what you hold in your mind's eye, take 2 minutes to visualize your board members, in the present tense and feel it in you heart as if the goal is already complete.

TOP THREE THINGS YOU ARE GREATFUL FOR:

1. _____
2. _____
3. _____

FOCUS ON YOUR ONE THING TODAY & TAKE MASSIVE ACTION!

"If you nurture your mind, body, and spirit, your time will expand. You will gain a new perspective that will allow you to accomplish much more."

—BRIAN KOSLOW

———————————

Here are the Traits of the GREATS required to choose your superstar board members:

- Integrity
- Honesty
- Loyalty
- Respectfulness
- Responsibility

- Humility
- Compassion
- Fairness
- Forgiveness
- Authenticity

Gratitude is key and visualizing in the present moment, exactly what you hold in your mind's eye, take 2 minutes to visualize your board members, in the present tense and feel it in you heart as if the goal is already complete.

TOP THREE THINGS YOU ARE GREATFUL FOR:

1. _____
2. _____
3. _____

FOCUS ON YOUR ONE THING TODAY & TAKE MASSIVE ACTION!

*"Failure is simply the opportunity to begin
again, this time more intelligently."*

—HENRY FORD

———————

Here are the Traits of the GREATS required to choose your superstar board members:

- Integrity
- Honesty
- Loyalty
- Respectfulness
- Responsibility

- Humility
- Compassion
- Fairness
- Forgiveness
- Authenticity

Gratitude is key and visualizing in the present moment, exactly what you hold in your mind's eye, take 2 minutes to visualize your board members, in the present tense and feel it in you heart as if the goal is already complete.

TOP THREE THINGS YOU ARE GREATFUL FOR:

1. _____
2. _____
3. _____

FOCUS ON YOUR ONE THING TODAY & TAKE MASSIVE ACTION!

"Success is where preparation and opportunity meet."

—BOBBY UNSER

Here are the Traits of the GREATS required to choose your superstar board members:

- Integrity
- Honesty
- Loyalty
- Respectfulness
- Responsibility

- Humility
- Compassion
- Fairness
- Forgiveness
- Authenticity

Gratitude is key and visualizing in the present moment, exactly what you hold in your mind's eye, take 2 minutes to visualize your board members, in the present tense and feel it in you heart as if the goal is already complete.

TOP THREE THINGS YOU ARE GREATFUL FOR:

1. _____
2. _____
3. _____

FOCUS ON YOUR ONE THING TODAY & TAKE MASSIVE ACTION!

"If opportunity doesn't knock, build a door."

—MILTON BERLE

Here are the Traits of the GREATS required to choose your superstar board members:

- Integrity
- Honesty
- Loyalty
- Respectfulness
- Responsibility

- Humility
- Compassion
- Fairness
- Forgiveness
- Authenticity

Gratitude is key and visualizing in the present moment, exactly what you hold in your mind's eye, take 2 minutes to visualize your board members, in the present tense and feel it in you heart as if the goal is already complete.

TOP THREE THINGS YOU ARE GREATFUL FOR:

1. _____
2. _____
3. _____

FOCUS ON YOUR ONE THING TODAY & TAKE MASSIVE ACTION!

"Outstanding people have one thing in common:
an absolute sense of mission."

—ZIG ZIGLAR

Here are the Traits of the GREATS required to choose your superstar board members:

- Integrity
- Honesty
- Loyalty
- Respectfulness
- Responsibility

- Humility
- Compassion
- Fairness
- Forgiveness
- Authenticity

Gratitude is key and visualizing in the present moment, exactly what you hold in your mind's eye, take 2 minutes to visualize your board members, in the present tense and feel it in you heart as if the goal is already complete.

TOP THREE THINGS YOU ARE GREATFUL FOR:

1. _____
2. _____
3. _____

FOCUS ON YOUR ONE THING TODAY & TAKE MASSIVE ACTION!

"Human beings are infinitely worth studying, especially the peculiarities that often go along with outstanding gifts."

—PAUL JOHNSON

———————

Here are the Traits of the GREATS required to choose your superstar board members:

- Integrity
- Honesty
- Loyalty
- Respectfulness
- Responsibility

- Humility
- Compassion
- Fairness
- Forgiveness
- Authenticity

Gratitude is key and visualizing in the present moment, exactly what you hold in your mind's eye, take 2 minutes to visualize your board members, in the present tense and feel it in you heart as if the goal is already complete.

TOP THREE THINGS YOU ARE GREATFUL FOR:

1. _____
2. _____
3. _____

FOCUS ON YOUR ONE THING TODAY & TAKE MASSIVE ACTION!

"The higher your energy level, the more efficient your body. The more efficient your body, the better you feel and the more you will use your talent to produce outstanding results."

—TONY ROBBINS

Here are the Traits of the GREATS required to choose your superstar board members:

- Integrity
- Honesty
- Loyalty
- Respectfulness
- Responsibility

- Humility
- Compassion
- Fairness
- Forgiveness
- Authenticity

Gratitude is key and visualizing in the present moment, exactly what you hold in your mind's eye, take 2 minutes to visualize your board members, in the present tense and feel it in you heart as if the goal is already complete.

TOP THREE THINGS YOU ARE GREATFUL FOR:

1. _____
2. _____
3. _____

FOCUS ON YOUR ONE THING TODAY & TAKE MASSIVE ACTION!

"Passion is one great force that unleashes creativity, because if you're passionate about something, then you're more willing to take risks."

—YO YO MA

———————

Here are the Traits of the GREATS required to choose your superstar board members:

- Integrity
- Honesty
- Loyalty
- Respectfulness
- Responsibility

- Humility
- Compassion
- Fairness
- Forgiveness
- Authenticity

Gratitude is key and visualizing in the present moment, exactly what you hold in your mind's eye, take 2 minutes to visualize your board members, in the present tense and feel it in you heart as if the goal is already complete.

TOP THREE THINGS YOU ARE GREATFUL FOR:

1. _____
2. _____
3. _____

FOCUS ON YOUR ONE THING TODAY & TAKE MASSIVE ACTION!

"Follow your passion, be prepared to work hard and sacrifice, and, above all, don't let anyone limit your dreams."

—DONOVAN BAILEY

Here are the Traits of the GREATS required to choose your superstar board members:

- Integrity
- Honesty
- Loyalty
- Respectfulness
- Responsibility

- Humility
- Compassion
- Fairness
- Forgiveness
- Authenticity

Gratitude is key and visualizing in the present moment, exactly what you hold in your mind's eye, take 2 minutes to visualize your board members, in the present tense and feel it in you heart as if the goal is already complete.

TOP THREE THINGS YOU ARE GREATFUL FOR:

1. _____
2. _____
3. _____

FOCUS ON YOUR ONE THING TODAY & TAKE MASSIVE ACTION!

*"Passion is energy. Feel the power that comes
from focusing on what excites you."*

—OPRAH WINFREY

———————

Here are the Traits of the GREATS required to choose your superstar board members:

- Integrity
- Honesty
- Loyalty
- Respectfulness
- Responsibility

- Humility
- Compassion
- Fairness
- Forgiveness
- Authenticity

Gratitude is key and visualizing in the present moment, exactly what you hold in your mind's eye, take 2 minutes to visualize your board members, in the present tense and feel it in you heart as if the goal is already complete.

TOP THREE THINGS YOU ARE GREATFUL FOR:

1. _____
2. _____
3. _____

FOCUS ON YOUR ONE THING TODAY & TAKE MASSIVE ACTION!

"Adopt the pace of nature: her secret is patience."

—RALPH WALDO EMERSON

———

Here are the Traits of the GREATS required to choose your superstar board members:

- Integrity
- Honesty
- Loyalty
- Respectfulness
- Responsibility

- Humility
- Compassion
- Fairness
- Forgiveness
- Authenticity

Gratitude is key and visualizing in the present moment, exactly what you hold in your mind's eye, take 2 minutes to visualize your board members, in the present tense and feel it in you heart as if the goal is already complete.

TOP THREE THINGS YOU ARE GREATFUL FOR:

1. _____
2. _____
3. _____

FOCUS ON YOUR ONE THING TODAY & TAKE MASSIVE ACTION!

"The two most powerful warriors are patience and time."

—LEO TOLSTOY

———

Here are the Traits of the GREATS required to choose your superstar board members:

- Integrity
- Honesty
- Loyalty
- Respectfulness
- Responsibility

- Humility
- Compassion
- Fairness
- Forgiveness
- Authenticity

Gratitude is key and visualizing in the present moment, exactly what you hold in your mind's eye, take 2 minutes to visualize your board members, in the present tense and feel it in you heart as if the goal is already complete.

TOP THREE THINGS YOU ARE GREATFUL FOR:

1. _____
2. _____
3. _____

FOCUS ON YOUR ONE THING TODAY & TAKE MASSIVE ACTION!

"Have patience. All things are difficult before they become easy."

—SAADI

Here are the Traits of the GREATS required to choose your superstar board members:

- Integrity
- Honesty
- Loyalty
- Respectfulness
- Responsibility

- Humility
- Compassion
- Fairness
- Forgiveness
- Authenticity

Gratitude is key and visualizing in the present moment, exactly what you hold in your mind's eye, take 2 minutes to visualize your board members, in the present tense and feel it in you heart as if the goal is already complete.

TOP THREE THINGS YOU ARE GREATFUL FOR:

1. _____

2. _____

3. _____

FOCUS ON YOUR ONE THING TODAY & TAKE MASSIVE ACTION!

*"Perseverance is the hard work you do after you get
tired of doing the hard work you already did."*

—NEWT GINGRICH

———————

Here are the Traits of the GREATS required to choose your superstar board members:

- Integrity
- Honesty
- Loyalty
- Respectfulness
- Responsibility

- Humility
- Compassion
- Fairness
- Forgiveness
- Authenticity

Gratitude is key and visualizing in the present moment, exactly what you hold in your mind's eye, take 2 minutes to visualize your board members, in the present tense and feel it in you heart as if the goal is already complete.

TOP THREE THINGS YOU ARE GREATFUL FOR:

1. _____
2. _____
3. _____

FOCUS ON YOUR ONE THING TODAY & TAKE MASSIVE ACTION!

"Perseverance is failing 19 times and succeeding the 20th."

—JULIE ANDREWS

———————

Here are the Traits of the GREATS required to choose your superstar board members:

- Integrity
- Honesty
- Loyalty
- Respectfulness
- Responsibility

- Humility
- Compassion
- Fairness
- Forgiveness
- Authenticity

Gratitude is key and visualizing in the present moment, exactly what you hold in your mind's eye, take 2 minutes to visualize your board members, in the present tense and feel it in you heart as if the goal is already complete.

TOP THREE THINGS YOU ARE GREATFUL FOR:

1. _____
2. _____
3. _____

FOCUS ON YOUR ONE THING TODAY & TAKE MASSIVE ACTION!

*"No one succeeds without effort . . . Those who
succeed owe their success to perseverance."*

—RAMANA MAHARSHI

Here are the Traits of the GREATS required to choose your superstar board members:

- Integrity
- Honesty
- Loyalty
- Respectfulness
- Responsibility

- Humility
- Compassion
- Fairness
- Forgiveness
- Authenticity

Gratitude is key and visualizing in the present moment, exactly what you hold in your mind's eye, take 2 minutes to visualize your board members, in the present tense and feel it in you heart as if the goal is already complete.

TOP THREE THINGS YOU ARE GREATFUL FOR:

1. _____
2. _____
3. _____

FOCUS ON YOUR ONE THING TODAY & TAKE MASSIVE ACTION!

"Practice does not make perfect. Only
perfect practice makes perfect."

—VINCE LOMBARDI

———————

Here are the Traits of the GREATS required to choose your superstar board members:

- Integrity
- Honesty
- Loyalty
- Respectfulness
- Responsibility

- Humility
- Compassion
- Fairness
- Forgiveness
- Authenticity

Gratitude is key and visualizing in the present moment, exactly what you hold in your mind's eye, take 2 minutes to visualize your board members, in the present tense and feel it in you heart as if the goal is already complete.

TOP THREE THINGS YOU ARE GREATFUL FOR:

1. _____
2. _____
3. _____

FOCUS ON YOUR ONE THING TODAY & TAKE MASSIVE ACTION!

"Everything is practice."

—PELE

———————

Here are the Traits of the GREATS required to choose your superstar board members:

- Integrity
- Honesty
- Loyalty
- Respectfulness
- Responsibility

- Humility
- Compassion
- Fairness
- Forgiveness
- Authenticity

Gratitude is key and visualizing in the present moment, exactly what you hold in your mind's eye, take 2 minutes to visualize your board members, in the present tense and feel it in you heart as if the goal is already complete.

TOP THREE THINGS YOU ARE GREATFUL FOR:

1. _____
2. _____
3. _____

FOCUS ON YOUR ONE THING TODAY & TAKE MASSIVE ACTION!

*"An ounce of practice is worth
more than tons of preaching."*

—MAHATMA GANDHI

———————

Here are the Traits of the GREATS required to choose your superstar board members:

- Integrity
- Honesty
- Loyalty
- Respectfulness
- Responsibility

- Humility
- Compassion
- Fairness
- Forgiveness
- Authenticity

Gratitude is key and visualizing in the present moment, exactly what you hold in your mind's eye, take 2 minutes to visualize your board members, in the present tense and feel it in you heart as if the goal is already complete.

TOP THREE THINGS YOU ARE GREATFUL FOR:

1. _____
2. _____
3. _____

FOCUS ON YOUR ONE THING TODAY & TAKE MASSIVE ACTION!

"The key is not to prioritize what's on your schedule, but to schedule your priorities."

—STEPHEN COVEY

———————

Here are the Traits of the GREATS required to choose your superstar board members:

- Integrity
- Honesty
- Loyalty
- Respectfulness
- Responsibility

- Humility
- Compassion
- Fairness
- Forgiveness
- Authenticity

Gratitude is key and visualizing in the present moment, exactly what you hold in your mind's eye, take 2 minutes to visualize your board members, in the present tense and feel it in you heart as if the goal is already complete.

TOP THREE THINGS YOU ARE GREATFUL FOR:

1. _____
2. _____
3. _____

FOCUS ON YOUR ONE THING TODAY & TAKE MASSIVE ACTION!

"Pursuit of perfection is futile. Instead, I prioritize and often realize goals or tasks I've been aiming for just aren't that important."

—AISHA TYLER

———————

Here are the Traits of the GREATS required to choose your superstar board members:

- Integrity
- Honesty
- Loyalty
- Respectfulness
- Responsibility

- Humility
- Compassion
- Fairness
- Forgiveness
- Authenticity

Gratitude is key and visualizing in the present moment, exactly what you hold in your mind's eye, take 2 minutes to visualize your board members, in the present tense and feel it in you heart as if the goal is already complete.

TOP THREE THINGS YOU ARE GREATFUL FOR:

1. _____
2. _____
3. _____

FOCUS ON YOUR ONE THING TODAY & TAKE MASSIVE ACTION!

"The best we can do is prioritize our
needs and make choices accordingly."

—JANET EVANOVICH

———————

Here are the Traits of the GREATS required to choose your superstar board members:

- Integrity
- Honesty
- Loyalty
- Respectfulness
- Responsibility

- Humility
- Compassion
- Fairness
- Forgiveness
- Authenticity

Gratitude is key and visualizing in the present moment, exactly what you hold in your mind's eye, take 2 minutes to visualize your board members, in the present tense and feel it in you heart as if the goal is already complete.

TOP THREE THINGS YOU ARE GREATFUL FOR:

1. _____

2. _____

3. _____

FOCUS ON YOUR ONE THING TODAY & TAKE MASSIVE ACTION!

"A wise man can learn more from a foolish question than a fool can learn from a wise answer."

—BRUCE LEE

———————

Here are the Traits of the GREATS required to choose your superstar board members:

- Integrity
- Honesty
- Loyalty
- Respectfulness
- Responsibility

- Humility
- Compassion
- Fairness
- Forgiveness
- Authenticity

Gratitude is key and visualizing in the present moment, exactly what you hold in your mind's eye, take 2 minutes to visualize your board members, in the present tense and feel it in you heart as if the goal is already complete.

TOP THREE THINGS YOU ARE GREATFUL FOR:

1. _____
2. _____
3. _____

FOCUS ON YOUR ONE THING TODAY & TAKE MASSIVE ACTION!

"Question everything. Learn something. Answer nothing."

—EURIPIDES

———————

Here are the Traits of the GREATS required to choose your superstar board members:

- Integrity
- Honesty
- Loyalty
- Respectfulness
- Responsibility

- Humility
- Compassion
- Fairness
- Forgiveness
- Authenticity

Gratitude is key and visualizing in the present moment, exactly what you hold in your mind's eye, take 2 minutes to visualize your board members, in the present tense and feel it in you heart as if the goal is already complete.

TOP THREE THINGS YOU ARE GREATFUL FOR:

1. _____
2. _____
3. _____

FOCUS ON YOUR ONE THING TODAY & TAKE MASSIVE ACTION!

*"By doubting we are led to question, by
questioning we arrive at the truth."*

—PETER ABELARD

Here are the Traits of the GREATS required to choose your superstar board members:

- Integrity
- Honesty
- Loyalty
- Respectfulness
- Responsibility

- Humility
- Compassion
- Fairness
- Forgiveness
- Authenticity

Gratitude is key and visualizing in the present moment, exactly what you hold in your mind's eye, take 2 minutes to visualize your board members, in the present tense and feel it in you heart as if the goal is already complete.

TOP THREE THINGS YOU ARE GREATFUL FOR:

1. _____
2. _____
3. _____

FOCUS ON YOUR ONE THING TODAY & TAKE MASSIVE ACTION!

*"By constant self-discipline and self-control you
can develop greatness of character."*

—GRENVILLE KLEISER

———————

Here are the Traits of the GREATS required to choose your superstar board members:

- Integrity
- Honesty
- Loyalty
- Respectfulness
- Responsibility

- Humility
- Compassion
- Fairness
- Forgiveness
- Authenticity

Gratitude is key and visualizing in the present moment, exactly what you hold in your mind's eye, take 2 minutes to visualize your board members, in the present tense and feel it in you heart as if the goal is already complete.

TOP THREE THINGS YOU ARE GREATFUL FOR:

1. _____
2. _____
3. _____

FOCUS ON YOUR ONE THING TODAY & TAKE MASSIVE ACTION!

"Emotional self-control is the result of hard work, not an inherent skill."

—TRAVIS BRADBERRY

Here are the Traits of the GREATS required to choose your superstar board members:

- Integrity
- Honesty
- Loyalty
- Respectfulness
- Responsibility

- Humility
- Compassion
- Fairness
- Forgiveness
- Authenticity

Gratitude is key and visualizing in the present moment, exactly what you hold in your mind's eye, take 2 minutes to visualize your board members, in the present tense and feel it in you heart as if the goal is already complete.

TOP THREE THINGS YOU ARE GREATFUL FOR:

1. _____
2. _____
3. _____

FOCUS ON YOUR ONE THING TODAY & TAKE MASSIVE ACTION!

"Self-control means wanting to be effective at some random point in the infinite radiations of my spiritual existence."

—FRANZ KAFKA

———————

Here are the Traits of the GREATS required to choose your superstar board members:

- Integrity
- Honesty
- Loyalty
- Respectfulness
- Responsibility

- Humility
- Compassion
- Fairness
- Forgiveness
- Authenticity

Gratitude is key and visualizing in the present moment, exactly what you hold in your mind's eye, take 2 minutes to visualize your board members, in the present tense and feel it in you heart as if the goal is already complete.

TOP THREE THINGS YOU ARE GREATFUL FOR:

1. _____
2. _____
3. _____

FOCUS ON YOUR ONE THING TODAY & TAKE MASSIVE ACTION!

*"It is possible to fly without motors, but
not without knowledge and skill."*

—WILBUR WRIGHT

Here are the Traits of the GREATS required to choose your superstar board members:

- Integrity
- Honesty
- Loyalty
- Respectfulness
- Responsibility

- Humility
- Compassion
- Fairness
- Forgiveness
- Authenticity

Gratitude is key and visualizing in the present moment, exactly what you hold in your mind's eye, take 2 minutes to visualize your board members, in the present tense and feel it in you heart as if the goal is already complete.

TOP THREE THINGS YOU ARE GREATFUL FOR:

1. _____
2. _____
3. _____

FOCUS ON YOUR ONE THING TODAY & TAKE MASSIVE ACTION!

"When love and skill work together,
expect a masterpiece."

—JOHN RUSKIN

———————

Here are the Traits of the GREATS required to choose your superstar board members:

- Integrity
- Honesty
- Loyalty
- Respectfulness
- Responsibility

- Humility
- Compassion
- Fairness
- Forgiveness
- Authenticity

Gratitude is key and visualizing in the present moment, exactly what you hold in your mind's eye, take 2 minutes to visualize your board members, in the present tense and feel it in you heart as if the goal is already complete.

TOP THREE THINGS YOU ARE GREATFUL FOR:

1. _____
2. _____
3. _____

FOCUS ON YOUR ONE THING TODAY & TAKE MASSIVE ACTION!

"Learning how to learn is life's most important skill."

—TONY BUZAN

———————

Here are the Traits of the GREATS required to choose your superstar board members:

- Integrity
- Honesty
- Loyalty
- Respectfulness
- Responsibility

- Humility
- Compassion
- Fairness
- Forgiveness
- Authenticity

Gratitude is key and visualizing in the present moment, exactly what you hold in your mind's eye, take 2 minutes to visualize your board members, in the present tense and feel it in you heart as if the goal is already complete.

TOP THREE THINGS YOU ARE GREATFUL FOR:

1. _____
2. _____
3. _____

FOCUS ON YOUR ONE THING TODAY & TAKE MASSIVE ACTION!

*"Share your smile with the world. It's
a symbol of friendship and peace."*

—CHRISTIE BRINKLEY

———————

Here are the Traits of the GREATS required to choose your superstar board members:

- Integrity
- Honesty
- Loyalty
- Respectfulness
- Responsibility

- Humility
- Compassion
- Fairness
- Forgiveness
- Authenticity

Gratitude is key and visualizing in the present moment, exactly what you hold in your mind's eye, take 2 minutes to visualize your board members, in the present tense and feel it in you heart as if the goal is already complete.

TOP THREE THINGS YOU ARE GREATFUL FOR:

1. _____
2. _____
3. _____

FOCUS ON YOUR ONE THING TODAY & TAKE MASSIVE ACTION!

"Beauty is power; a smile is its sword."

—JOHN RAY

———————

Here are the Traits of the GREATS required to choose your superstar board members:

- Integrity
- Honesty
- Loyalty
- Respectfulness
- Responsibility

- Humility
- Compassion
- Fairness
- Forgiveness
- Authenticity

Gratitude is key and visualizing in the present moment, exactly what you hold in your mind's eye, take 2 minutes to visualize your board members, in the present tense and feel it in you heart as if the goal is already complete.

TOP THREE THINGS YOU ARE GREATFUL FOR:

1. _____
2. _____
3. _____

FOCUS ON YOUR ONE THING TODAY & TAKE MASSIVE ACTION!

"Nothing you wear is more important than your smile."

—CONNIE STEVENS

———————

Here are the Traits of the GREATS required to choose your superstar board members:

- Integrity
- Honesty
- Loyalty
- Respectfulness
- Responsibility

- Humility
- Compassion
- Fairness
- Forgiveness
- Authenticity

Gratitude is key and visualizing in the present moment, exactly what you hold in your mind's eye, take 2 minutes to visualize your board members, in the present tense and feel it in you heart as if the goal is already complete.

TOP THREE THINGS YOU ARE GREATFUL FOR:

1. _____
2. _____
3. _____

FOCUS ON YOUR ONE THING TODAY & TAKE MASSIVE ACTION!

*"Failure will never overtake me if my determination
to succeed is strong enough."*

—OG MANDINO

———————

Here are the Traits of the GREATS required to choose your superstar board members:

- Integrity
- Honesty
- Loyalty
- Respectfulness
- Responsibility

- Humility
- Compassion
- Fairness
- Forgiveness
- Authenticity

Gratitude is key and visualizing in the present moment, exactly what you hold in your mind's eye, take 2 minutes to visualize your board members, in the present tense and feel it in you heart as if the goal is already complete.

TOP THREE THINGS YOU ARE GREATFUL FOR:

1. _____
2. _____
3. _____

FOCUS ON YOUR ONE THING TODAY & TAKE MASSIVE ACTION!

"In order to succeed, we must first believe that we can."

—NIKOS KAZANTZAKIS

———————

Here are the Traits of the GREATS required to choose your superstar board members:

- Integrity
- Honesty
- Loyalty
- Respectfulness
- Responsibility

- Humility
- Compassion
- Fairness
- Forgiveness
- Authenticity

Gratitude is key and visualizing in the present moment, exactly what you hold in your mind's eye, take 2 minutes to visualize your board members, in the present tense and feel it in you heart as if the goal is already complete.

TOP THREE THINGS YOU ARE GREATFUL FOR:

1. _____
2. _____
3. _____

FOCUS ON YOUR ONE THING TODAY & TAKE MASSIVE ACTION!

"However difficult life may seem, there is always something you can do and succeed at."

—STEPHEN HAWKING

Here are the Traits of the GREATS required to choose your superstar board members:

- Integrity
- Honesty
- Loyalty
- Respectfulness
- Responsibility

- Humility
- Compassion
- Fairness
- Forgiveness
- Authenticity

Gratitude is key and visualizing in the present moment, exactly what you hold in your mind's eye, take 2 minutes to visualize your board members, in the present tense and feel it in you heart as if the goal is already complete.

TOP THREE THINGS YOU ARE GREATFUL FOR:

1. _____
2. _____
3. _____

FOCUS ON YOUR ONE THING TODAY & TAKE MASSIVE ACTION!

*"Think like a queen. A queen is not afraid to fail.
Failure is another stepping stone to greatness."*

—OPRAH WINFREY

———————

Here are the Traits of the GREATS required to choose your superstar board members:

- Integrity
- Honesty
- Loyalty
- Respectfulness
- Responsibility

- Humility
- Compassion
- Fairness
- Forgiveness
- Authenticity

Gratitude is key and visualizing in the present moment, exactly what you hold in your mind's eye, take 2 minutes to visualize your board members, in the present tense and feel it in you heart as if the goal is already complete.

TOP THREE THINGS YOU ARE GREATFUL FOR:

1. _____
2. _____
3. _____

FOCUS ON YOUR ONE THING TODAY & TAKE MASSIVE ACTION!

"When you think positive, good things happen."

—MATT KEMP

———————

Here are the Traits of the GREATS required to choose your superstar board members:

- Integrity
- Honesty
- Loyalty
- Respectfulness
- Responsibility

- Humility
- Compassion
- Fairness
- Forgiveness
- Authenticity

Gratitude is key and visualizing in the present moment, exactly what you hold in your mind's eye, take 2 minutes to visualize your board members, in the present tense and feel it in you heart as if the goal is already complete.

TOP THREE THINGS YOU ARE GREATFUL FOR:

1. _____
2. _____
3. _____

FOCUS ON YOUR ONE THING TODAY & TAKE MASSIVE ACTION!

"Think in the morning. Act in the noon.
Eat in the evening. Sleep in the night."

—WILLIAM BLAKE

———————

Here are the Traits of the GREATS required to choose your superstar board members:

- Integrity
- Honesty
- Loyalty
- Respectfulness
- Responsibility

- Humility
- Compassion
- Fairness
- Forgiveness
- Authenticity

Gratitude is key and visualizing in the present moment, exactly what you hold in your mind's eye, take 2 minutes to visualize your board members, in the present tense and feel it in you heart as if the goal is already complete.

TOP THREE THINGS YOU ARE GREATFUL FOR:

1. _____
2. _____
3. _____

FOCUS ON YOUR ONE THING TODAY & TAKE MASSIVE ACTION!

"Love all, trust a few, do wrong to none."

—WILLIAM SHAKESPEARE

———————

Here are the Traits of the GREATS required to choose your superstar board members:

- Integrity
- Honesty
- Loyalty
- Respectfulness
- Responsibility

- Humility
- Compassion
- Fairness
- Forgiveness
- Authenticity

Gratitude is key and visualizing in the present moment, exactly what you hold in your mind's eye, take 2 minutes to visualize your board members, in the present tense and feel it in you heart as if the goal is already complete.

TOP THREE THINGS YOU ARE GREATFUL FOR:

1. _____
2. _____
3. _____

FOCUS ON YOUR ONE THING TODAY & TAKE MASSIVE ACTION!

"Trust yourself, you know more than you think you do."

—BENJAMIN SPOCK

———————

Here are the Traits of the GREATS required to choose your superstar board members:

- Integrity
- Honesty
- Loyalty
- Respectfulness
- Responsibility

- Humility
- Compassion
- Fairness
- Forgiveness
- Authenticity

Gratitude is key and visualizing in the present moment, exactly what you hold in your mind's eye, take 2 minutes to visualize your board members, in the present tense and feel it in you heart as if the goal is already complete.

TOP THREE THINGS YOU ARE GREATFUL FOR:

1. _____
2. _____
3. _____

FOCUS ON YOUR ONE THING TODAY & TAKE MASSIVE ACTION!

*"Trust in dreams, for in them is
hidden the gate to eternity."*

—KHALIL GIBRAN

———————

Here are the Traits of the GREATS required to choose your superstar board members:

- Integrity
- Honesty
- Loyalty
- Respectfulness
- Responsibility

- Humility
- Compassion
- Fairness
- Forgiveness
- Authenticity

Gratitude is key and visualizing in the present moment, exactly what you hold in your mind's eye, take 2 minutes to visualize your board members, in the present tense and feel it in you heart as if the goal is already complete.

TOP THREE THINGS YOU ARE GREATFUL FOR:

1. _____
2. _____
3. _____

FOCUS ON YOUR ONE THING TODAY & TAKE MASSIVE ACTION!

"One of the most beautiful qualities of true friendship
is to understand and to be understood."

—LUCIUS ANNAEUS SENECA

———————

Here are the Traits of the GREATS required to choose your superstar board members:

- Integrity
- Honesty
- Loyalty
- Respectfulness
- Responsibility

- Humility
- Compassion
- Fairness
- Forgiveness
- Authenticity

Gratitude is key and visualizing in the present moment, exactly what you hold in your mind's eye, take 2 minutes to visualize your board members, in the present tense and feel it in you heart as if the goal is already complete.

TOP THREE THINGS YOU ARE GREATFUL FOR:

1. _____
2. _____
3. _____

FOCUS ON YOUR ONE THING TODAY & TAKE MASSIVE ACTION!

"Mystery creates wonder, and wonder is the
basis of man's desire to understand."

—NEIL ARMSTRONG

———————

Here are the Traits of the GREATS required to choose your superstar board members:

- Integrity
- Honesty
- Loyalty
- Respectfulness
- Responsibility

- Humility
- Compassion
- Fairness
- Forgiveness
- Authenticity

Gratitude is key and visualizing in the present moment, exactly what you hold in your mind's eye, take 2 minutes to visualize your board members, in the present tense and feel it in you heart as if the goal is already complete.

TOP THREE THINGS YOU ARE GREATFUL FOR:

1. _____
2. _____
3. _____

FOCUS ON YOUR ONE THING TODAY & TAKE MASSIVE ACTION!

"If you can't explain it simply, you don't understand it well enough."

—ALBERT EINSTEIN

———————

Here are the Traits of the GREATS required to choose your superstar board members:

- Integrity
- Honesty
- Loyalty
- Respectfulness
- Responsibility

- Humility
- Compassion
- Fairness
- Forgiveness
- Authenticity

Gratitude is key and visualizing in the present moment, exactly what you hold in your mind's eye, take 2 minutes to visualize your board members, in the present tense and feel it in you heart as if the goal is already complete.

TOP THREE THINGS YOU ARE GREATFUL FOR:

1. _____
2. _____
3. _____

FOCUS ON YOUR ONE THING TODAY & TAKE MASSIVE ACTION!

"Try not to become a man of success, but rather try to become a man of value."

—ALBERT EINSTEIN

———————

Here are the Traits of the GREATS required to choose your superstar board members:

- Integrity
- Honesty
- Loyalty
- Respectfulness
- Responsibility

- Humility
- Compassion
- Fairness
- Forgiveness
- Authenticity

Gratitude is key and visualizing in the present moment, exactly what you hold in your mind's eye, take 2 minutes to visualize your board members, in the present tense and feel it in you heart as if the goal is already complete.

TOP THREE THINGS YOU ARE GREATFUL FOR:

1. _____
2. _____
3. _____

FOCUS ON YOUR ONE THING TODAY & TAKE MASSIVE ACTION!

"Price is what you pay. Value is what you get."

—WARREN BUFFET

———————

Here are the Traits of the GREATS required to choose your superstar board members:

- Integrity
- Honesty
- Loyalty
- Respectfulness
- Responsibility

- Humility
- Compassion
- Fairness
- Forgiveness
- Authenticity

Gratitude is key and visualizing in the present moment, exactly what you hold in your mind's eye, take 2 minutes to visualize your board members, in the present tense and feel it in you heart as if the goal is already complete.

TOP THREE THINGS YOU ARE GREATFUL FOR:

1. _____
2. _____
3. _____

FOCUS ON YOUR ONE THING TODAY & TAKE MASSIVE ACTION!

*"The value of life can be measured by how many
times your soul has been deeply stirred."*

—SOICHIRO HONDA

———————

Here are the Traits of the GREATS required to choose your superstar board members:

- Integrity
- Honesty
- Loyalty
- Respectfulness
- Responsibility

- Humility
- Compassion
- Fairness
- Forgiveness
- Authenticity

Gratitude is key and visualizing in the present moment, exactly what you hold in your mind's eye, take 2 minutes to visualize your board members, in the present tense and feel it in you heart as if the goal is already complete.

TOP THREE THINGS YOU ARE GREATFUL FOR:

1. _____
2. _____
3. _____

FOCUS ON YOUR ONE THING TODAY & TAKE MASSIVE ACTION!

*"You were born to win, but to be a winner, you must
plan to win, prepare to win, and expect to win."*

—ZIG ZIGLAR

———————————

Here are the Traits of the GREATS required to choose your superstar board members:

- Integrity
- Honesty
- Loyalty
- Respectfulness
- Responsibility

- Humility
- Compassion
- Fairness
- Forgiveness
- Authenticity

Gratitude is key and visualizing in the present moment, exactly what you hold in your mind's eye, take 2 minutes to visualize your board members, in the present tense and feel it in you heart as if the goal is already complete.

TOP THREE THINGS YOU ARE GREATFUL FOR:

1. _____
2. _____
3. _____

FOCUS ON YOUR ONE THING TODAY & TAKE MASSIVE ACTION!

"Self-praise is for losers. Be a winner. Stand for something. Always have class, and be humble."

—JOHN MADDEN

Here are the Traits of the GREATS required to choose your superstar board members:

- Integrity
- Honesty
- Loyalty
- Respectfulness
- Responsibility

- Humility
- Compassion
- Fairness
- Forgiveness
- Authenticity

Gratitude is key and visualizing in the present moment, exactly what you hold in your mind's eye, take 2 minutes to visualize your board members, in the present tense and feel it in you heart as if the goal is already complete.

TOP THREE THINGS YOU ARE GREATFUL FOR:

1. _____
2. _____
3. _____

FOCUS ON YOUR ONE THING TODAY & TAKE MASSIVE ACTION!

"A winner never stops trying."

—TOM LANDRY

———————

Here are the Traits of the GREATS required to choose your superstar board members:

- Integrity
- Honesty
- Loyalty
- Respectfulness
- Responsibility

- Humility
- Compassion
- Fairness
- Forgiveness
- Authenticity

Gratitude is key and visualizing in the present moment, exactly what you hold in your mind's eye, take 2 minutes to visualize your board members, in the present tense and feel it in you heart as if the goal is already complete.

TOP THREE THINGS YOU ARE GREATFUL FOR:

1. _____
2. _____
3. _____

FOCUS ON YOUR ONE THING TODAY & TAKE MASSIVE ACTION!

*"The only true wisdom is in
knowing you know nothing."*

—SOCRATES

———————

Here are the Traits of the GREATS required to choose your superstar board members:

- Integrity
- Honesty
- Loyalty
- Respectfulness
- Responsibility

- Humility
- Compassion
- Fairness
- Forgiveness
- Authenticity

Gratitude is key and visualizing in the present moment, exactly what you hold in your mind's eye, take 2 minutes to visualize your board members, in the present tense and feel it in you heart as if the goal is already complete.

TOP THREE THINGS YOU ARE GREATFUL FOR:

1. _____

2. _____

3. _____

FOCUS ON YOUR ONE THING TODAY & TAKE MASSIVE ACTION!

"Science is organized knowledge.
Wisdom is organized life."

—IMMANUEL KANT

———————

Here are the Traits of the GREATS required to choose your superstar board members:

- Integrity
- Honesty
- Loyalty
- Respectfulness
- Responsibility

- Humility
- Compassion
- Fairness
- Forgiveness
- Authenticity

Gratitude is key and visualizing in the present moment, exactly what you hold in your mind's eye, take 2 minutes to visualize your board members, in the present tense and feel it in you heart as if the goal is already complete.

TOP THREE THINGS YOU ARE GREATFUL FOR:

1. _____
2. _____
3. _____

FOCUS ON YOUR ONE THING TODAY & TAKE MASSIVE ACTION!

"Silence is true wisdom's best reply."

—EURIPIDES

———————

Here are the Traits of the GREATS required to choose your superstar board members:

- Integrity
- Honesty
- Loyalty
- Respectfulness
- Responsibility

- Humility
- Compassion
- Fairness
- Forgiveness
- Authenticity

Gratitude is key and visualizing in the present moment, exactly what you hold in your mind's eye, take 2 minutes to visualize your board members, in the present tense and feel it in you heart as if the goal is already complete.

TOP THREE THINGS YOU ARE GREATFUL FOR:

1. _____
2. _____
3. _____

FOCUS ON YOUR ONE THING TODAY & TAKE MASSIVE ACTION!

"Zeal will do more than knowledge."

—WILLIAM HAZLITT

———————

Here are the Traits of the GREATS required to choose your superstar board members:

- Integrity
- Honesty
- Loyalty
- Respectfulness
- Responsibility

- Humility
- Compassion
- Fairness
- Forgiveness
- Authenticity

Gratitude is key and visualizing in the present moment, exactly what you hold in your mind's eye, take 2 minutes to visualize your board members, in the present tense and feel it in you heart as if the goal is already complete.

TOP THREE THINGS YOU ARE GREATFUL FOR:

1. _____
2. _____
3. _____

FOCUS ON YOUR ONE THING TODAY & TAKE MASSIVE ACTION!

"Zeal without knowledge is fire without light."

—THOMAS FULLER

Here are the Traits of the GREATS required to choose your superstar board members:

- Integrity
- Honesty
- Loyalty
- Respectfulness
- Responsibility

- Humility
- Compassion
- Fairness
- Forgiveness
- Authenticity

Gratitude is key and visualizing in the present moment, exactly what you hold in your mind's eye, take 2 minutes to visualize your board members, in the present tense and feel it in you heart as if the goal is already complete.

TOP THREE THINGS YOU ARE GREATFUL FOR:

1. _____
2. _____
3. _____

FOCUS ON YOUR ONE THING TODAY & TAKE MASSIVE ACTION!

*"Zeal is a volcano, the peak of which the grass
of indecisiveness does not grow."*

—KHALIL GIBRAN

———————

Here are the Traits of the GREATS required to choose your superstar board members:

- Integrity
- Honesty
- Loyalty
- Respectfulness
- Responsibility

- Humility
- Compassion
- Fairness
- Forgiveness
- Authenticity

Gratitude is key and visualizing in the present moment, exactly what you hold in your mind's eye, take 2 minutes to visualize your board members, in the present tense and feel it in you heart as if the goal is already complete.

TOP THREE THINGS YOU ARE GREATFUL FOR:

1. _____
2. _____
3. _____

FOCUS ON YOUR ONE THING TODAY & TAKE MASSIVE ACTION!

www.ingramcontent.com/pod-product-compliance
Lightning Source LLC
Chambersburg PA
CBHW072151090426
42740CB00012B/2224